GHOST PINE
ALL STORIES TRUE

GHOST PINE
ALL STORIES TRUE

Jeff Miller

Invisible Publishing

Halifax & Toronto

For Spike

Library and Archives Canada Cataloguing in Publication

Miller, Jeff, 1979-
    Ghost pine : all stories true / by Jeff Miller.

ISBN 978-1-926743-04-2

    1. Miller, Jeff, 1979-. 2. Youth--Québec (Province)--Montréal.
3. Authors, Canadian (English)--21st century--Biography. I. Title.

PS8626.I4495Z53 2010   C813'.6 C2010-901602-5

Designed by Megan Fildes
Cover illustration/Design by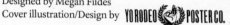

Typeset in Laurentian and Slate by Megan Fildes
With thanks to type designer Rod McDonald

Printed and bound in Canada

Invisible Publishing
Halifax & Toronto
www.invisiblepublishing.com

We acknowledge the support of the Canada Council for the Arts which last year invested $20.1 million in writing and publishing throughout Canada.

Invisible Publishing recognizes the support of the Province of Nova Scotia through the Department of Tourism, Culture & Heritage. We are pleased to work in partnership with the Culture Division to develop and promote our cultural resources for all Nova Scotians.

NOVA SCOTIA
Tourism, Culture and Heritage

Canada Council   Conseil des Arts
for the Arts   du Canada

I know what you're thinking, people should file their childhood
under "W" for "Who Cares?," but the mind must attend to the things
it is just beginning to understand, like how after all that fierce planning
I could grow up to be the soft ineffectual synthesis
of untold compromises that I am today.

David Berman, "The High Numbers"

PREFACE

THIS BOOK IS BOTH A COLLECTION OF SHORT STORIES AND AN archival document of the thirteen years I have published my zine *Ghost Pine* (originally *Otaku*), where these stories first appeared.

I began the zine when I was sixteen years old. I never intended to publish a zine for over a decade, but once I got over the initial terror of putting out the first issue I felt that I might be able to make another. There was never a master plan, I just wrote one story and then the next. Zines, then as now, take many forms but mine was always a collection of true short stories. This book contains the gold. It is a selection of the best stories from the past thirteen years. They are not organized chronologically; stories from the earliest issues are interspersed with later ones, bringing to light some of the major themes that have preoccupied my writing over the years. The original publication date of each story is noted for those who are interested.

Writers are often portrayed as solitary types, but my work has been produced within an international community of thousands of other zines. I read about them in newsprint punk magazines *Maximumrocknroll*, *HeartattaCk* and *Slug & Lettuce* and I sent away for hundreds over the years. I exchanged letters with dozens of young writers who published zines and developed deep friendships with some. Closer to home I have participated in a vibrant community of zine makers in both

Ottawa and Montreal. Some of the stories that appear in this collection were originally published in the zines of my friends.

Ghost Pine has no mainstream distribution; I have sold over ten thousand copies in person and through small independent distributors and bookstores. Despite this clandestine nature I always tried to make my stories accessible to all. I am always happiest when someone from outside my own community tells me that they have read and enjoyed my zine.

Despite this impulse toward accessibility I've tried to remain true to my life, which has not been without its rough patches or questionable behaviour. My mother still refuses to read the zine because of its salty language. Being true to life meant writing about my close relationship with my grandparents as much as it was about writing about the punk scene that I grew up in. It meant writing about loneliness as well as romance.

Anything could find its way into one of my pocket-sized zines, as long as it fit *Ghost Pine*'s motto: All Stories True.

Jeff Miller,

Montreal, 2010

1

"SIN CITY"

THE CITY OF MONTREAL IS HOME TO MILES OF SUBTERRANEAN boulevards know as the Underground City. They are a confusing warren of tunnels that run just beneath the department stores, strip clubs and movie theatres that line the parallel streets of Ste. Catherine and De Maisonneuve.

The corridors were excavated alongside the subway tunnels during the sixties and they stretch out labyrinthine from Metro stations. The architects envisioned Parisian-style boulevards running in trenches beneath the fair ville. Unfortunately, they did not turn out quite as planned and there are none of brasseries and couturiers that were in the original sketches and maquettes.

Instead they form an underworld where the utopic vision of the planners quickly gave way to the needs of the underground train's harried travelers. Here the commuter's motto of Not Enough Time has been turned into an aesthetic. Ninety-nine cent pizza parlours, dollar stores and tiny one-chair hair salons have colonized the underground streets. In the newsstands and tiny coffee kiosks that line the corridors, muffins are plentiful for those morning train riders without enough time to eat breakfast. When the rush of day gives way to the calm night, the stores pull down their steel blinds and scraps of newspaper blow down the tunnels on waves of subway-pushed air.

Culture, as well as commerce, burrowed its way underground. By day musicians perform beneath blue signs bearing the image of a white lyre. These denote areas where busking is authorized by the Societé de Transport de Montréal. At six in the morning the buskers line up at the STM office, crusty-eyed and hoping they're in time to claim a time slot in front of a lyre. These permits for the stations downtown are doled out on a first come first served basis.

In the musty, beige brick tunnels that I walk from the subway platform to work I sometimes see a silver-haired woman playing acoustic guitar. She sings the old sixties ballads of freedom in a saccharine voice. Other mornings I pass a man wearing dark glasses, tinkling the theme songs of popular soap operas on his Casio keyboard. His polyester gig bag, despite the early hour, is always littered with spare change. A copy of his self-produced CD sits next to the constellations of coins and features a colour-photocopied photograph of his face in the jewel case. A makeshift sign, written in sharpie on piece of loose leaf next to the disc, reads "10 songs, $15."

One Thursday after work, as I walked toward my train, I heard the high pitched twang of a guitar, its player calling out the lyrics to the Appalachian ballad "John Henry". "They laid poor John Henry in his grave," he howled, "Lord, lord, they laid poor John Henry in his grave."

I made my way down the passage, slowly approaching the singer. He was dressed not like one of the coal miners who originally sang the song, but instead wore blue jeans, sneakers and a flannel shirt. Strapped around his neck wasn't a guitar but a dobro, with a silver plate across the front. I watched him closely as he sang. He did not play in the reserved manner of the veteran subway musicians, but with real passion. His voice cracked when he sang the high notes and his fingers, encased in picks, scraped the tune out of his twangy instrument.

I didn't see Katie coming down the tunnel toward me until we literally ran into each other. "I was so amazed by this guy that I didn't see you," she said.

"Me too. It's really rare to hear good music in the subway."

Every week Katie and I met in the tunnel. We crossed paths in the spare minutes before her weekly acupuncture appointment and before I got on a train home after work.

The sheer size of the city of Montreal often makes it difficult for me to see my friends on a regular basis. Everyone is scattered in different *quartiers*, busy with work and the obsessions they are working to feed: graduate degrees, bands, art, drugs, love, or often more than one of the above. Metro doors will open to reveal a friend on the platform who just happens to have the afternoon off like you do. You have to capitalize on those rare moments by going for coffee together around the block and catching up. Plot, scheme and raise a caffeinated toast to the city that brought you together after keeping you apart for so long.

"Today I performed my dance piece!" Katie said, her eyes shimmering like lake water.

The previous week she had told me of a project for one of her dance classes. It was performed on the second floor of the Polish restaurant where she works as a waiter.

"It went really well," she said. She tied her dark hair back into a pony tail as she explained how the piece had been only half choreographed and the rest improvised. At uneven intervals as she performed, she would stop dancing and bus tables or receive impromptu Polish lessons from the restaurant's aged patriarch.

As a choreographer working as a waiter, Katie decided to marry the two forms of motion. She bridged the gap between her job and her art, as if waiting tables was just research on a certain type of movement.

It makes me wonder what I have taken from my job. Other than the stink on my hands that comes from cutting hunks of pink flesh on the meat-slicer all day, I don't know. I've been at my job long enough that I can make sandwiches, fill cardboard coffee cups, answer the telephone in French, take lunch orders, serve three customers at once and all the while chat about the Habs' latest defeat with a regular. I move without thinking but, unlike Katie, I lack the skills to turn my dance behind the deli counter into even the most rudimentary art. All I have to show for my work are my hands, a collection of scars in various states of healing after meat-cutting accidents of differing severity.

"I'm about to sing real loud. I hope you guys don't mind," said the dobro picker behind us, after having politely waited quite some time for us to finish our conversation.

"No, don't worry. We think you're great," I replied.

"Thanks." He strummed the first chord of a song, then stopped. "Your praise is like much needed water for a thirsty plant."

We stood and listened to him for a while, until Katie realized the time. "I've gotta go," she said, "I'm late!" She hugged me and was off down the tunnel. As I resumed my path in the opposite direction, the bluegrass player's song echoed after me.

The next Friday I grinned like a fool when, after more than a week's absence, I saw that the dobro picker was back. I dropped a loonie in his guitar case and leaned on the wall nearby. He sang a country-fried rendition of a Velvet Underground song, a wide smile upon his face.

After finishing his song he offered me a hand, his fingers ringed in silver picks. "My name's Terry," he said. "You were here last week, weren't you?" he asked.

I nodded and introduced myself. "I'm really glad you're here. Work nearly killed me today."

He looked at me thoughtfully. "Sometimes when I got depressed at my old job I used to go to the Multimags across the street. I liked looking at that *Easy Riders* magazine. You know the one with the, uh," he paused, "motorcycles? That used to cheer me right up, make it easier to get through the day."

I laughed, remembering the bikini-clad women draped over classic American motorcycles in the one or two issues of the magazine I had seen. A few *Easy Riders* pull-out posters of women with orange tanned skin had adorned the basement bedroom walls of one of my pubescent friends circa 1992.

"Just lookin' at the bikes right?"

"Yeah," he chuckled.

"Know any Gram Parsons songs?" I asked. The freshly-cashed pay cheque in my wallet and the prospect of a few days of rest after a punishing week cheered me.

"Hell yeah," he said, beginning to pluck the guitar line to

"Sin City." "Ah shit, what's the first line?"

"This old town is filled with sin / it will swallow you in..." I supplied.

The tune was long out of practice but he persisted. Terry sang the verses, humming when unsure of the lyrics, and I joined in on the chorus. "This old earthquake's gonna leave me in the poorhouse," I croaked, "it seems that this whole town's insane..."

Afternoon commuters and shoppers strode by, paying little attention. A pair of ragged voices were the soundtrack to another work week's slow fade to black.

(Ghost Pine #8: Wolf, 2004)

NOAH AND SNOW

"SO I WAS WALKING DOWN ST. LAURENT LAST NIGHT AND I DID something I don't usually do," Noah said.

"What's that?"

"Well, I guess I tried to pick a fight with somebody."

"What?"

"Well yeah, this big ape of a dude with a fancy leather jacket, Tommy Hilfiger jeans and gelled up hair was talking on a cell phone and as he was crossing the street he bumped into me."

"Uh huh."

"So I guess I said 'Why don't you go shove that cell phone up your ass.' We were walking at the same pace on either side of the street yelling insults back and forth for about five minutes, until he says to the person he's talking to, 'I'm going across the street to see what this motherfucker wants.'

"So he comes across the street at me and says 'Why don't you tell my brother what you were calling me' and hands me the phone, but it's dead. There's no one on the other end. So I hand it back to him and he says into it, 'Yeah, this guy thinks he's funny but really he just has nice eyes.'"

"Was he trying to hit on you?"

"No. Then he asks me if I have any smokes, and I do because

someone left these Japanese cigarettes at my house, but neither one of us has a light. So we start walking north again, next
to each other but not really together, you know. Then we see
this really angry kid, couldn't be older than fourteen, walking
down the street punching the wall.

"We ask him if he has a light, and he says 'I have fire for you,
if you got a smoke for me.' So we're all standing around smoking Japanese cigarettes on the sidewalk together. And then it
began to snow. The first snow of the year.

"When he finished his butt the kid took off. But me and the
cell phone guy stood and talked, only for a minute, but it was
a real quality conversation. You know?"

"I guess you should try to pick fights more often."

"Yeah, I guess." Noah sipped his tea.

(Fish Piss Vol. 3 #1, 2004)

ANOTHER DAY AT THE OFFICE

AFTER A FULL YEAR OF WRITING, NAIL BITING, AND TRACKING
down submissions Chris had finally finished his tape compila-
tion and the zine that went with it. It stood as the only document of some great local bands who had come and gone all
too quickly in the past few years. Soon we'd have Chris's tape
comp to help our fading memories.

As Chris ironed out the final details of his masterpiece I sat
on the stoop, read my book and pet the cat. The book I was
reading was a science fiction novel from the seventies, it was
about an anarchist utopian society. Just like the USSR after
1917 the anarchists in the book developed their own language
where "work" and "play" were the same word. I folded the
page back and threw the paperback into my bag. It was midnight, time to get to work.

Chris was anxious to print up the zine, in a mad dash for
completion before he skipped the continent for the rest of
the summer. Along with some last minute lay-outs, Chris had
mapped out our dubious bike route all the way across town to

the late-night copy shop.

"Well, we're going down the Prescott Highway, it's Monday so there won't be that many drunk drivers and luckily most of the drunks will be my co-workers who'll hit us but won't kill us. So make sure you're on that shoulder boy!"

So off we went. South across town on the Prescott Highway, past the industrial park on Colonnade, past the straight rows of pine trees that pass for re-forestation in these parts, stopping for a break just long enough to spit on the offices of the Ottawa *Sun*, past the motels in pine groves with buzzing neon signs, past the short glass towers owned by start-up computer companies, past the old airport drive-in and all the nearby vacant lots filled only by lonely hot dog stands and chip-wagons, past the airport itself, until finally, after a few too many near-death encounters with big rigs, we arrived at a strip-mall so long that it's impossible to see one end from the other, even on a smog-free night.

There was just enough time for coffee at Denny's. As soon as we enter we proceed to be berated by a gauntlet of Monday night drunks. I find myself promising once more to make Chris quit smoking. You see, Denny's alone isn't a magnet for assholes of all creeds and colours, it is only the smoking section that's filled with jerks twenty-four hours a day, while the non-smoking section remains empty, almost as a slap in the face to me.

We bike over to the copy depot, get buzzed in through the security door and settle in for a night's work. Work, yes, but play too, just like the ideal in my anarchist sci-fi paperback. Under the harsh fluorescent lights we are redefining what work can and should be. We are no longer defined by our jobs as dishwashers and tour guides on the lowest rung of the economic ladder. We are now writers and artists, editors and musicians whose skills are indispensable to our communities. We are taking risks to bring our art to the fore of our lives.

Romantic? Yeah, but we can't deny our four a.m. delusions of grandeur without ripping up our best intentions.

Slaving over copy machines I've noticed how much work

goes into the minute details. One small mistake and every-thing falls apart.

But soon the sun's harbinger began to push back the corners of night. The sky was the colour of bruises and the highway was abandoned as we traced our way home. Giddy with drowsiness, caffeine, and the endless possibilities of empty roads.

We pulled up to Chris's before sunrise but under final in-spection it looked like the whole batch was tainted by a tiny mistake in pagination. It was not only the waste of a night's work, but a whole preceding year of late night and early morning work and probably a year's worth of thought before he wrote a single word. Not to mention the countless cups of coffee and cigarettes that staved off sleep and hunger when inspiration hit.

We're doomed by the fact that our art is all process; people who read the zine seldom see the cogs. How biking an hour to the copy shop, getting called fags by South Keys assholes and standing under painfully bright lights inhaling copy toner are various art forms we've refined and nearly mastered. Our medium is our message, our art is as flawed and impermanent as our lives.

So, a flawed batch of zines, nothing a few more coffee-and-cigarette-fuelled nights couldn't take care of.

The sun poked a little higher in the five a.m. sky. Before I headed for home Chris and I shared a hug and a sigh.

"Another day at the office," I said as my bicycle carried me home.

(Otaku #5, 1999)

WHO'S THE GHOST?

I WASN'T ALWAYS THIS WAY. THERE WAS A TIME WHEN I WAS FULLY visible twenty-four hours a day.

Then one night he showed up in one of my dreams and tried to reason with me. He wore an Italian suit and had slicked-back hair. His watch was diamond encrusted and he looked at it impatiently as he talked to me.

"I've heard about you," I told him, "but I never thought you would come for me."

"Listen kid, I come for everyone. You think you're the only punk-ass that didn't get in line? Jesus Christ. Now quit wasting my time and sign these papers."

From an alligator skin briefcase he produced a ream of paper ten inches thick. "This is the contract. Everyone signs this. Once you ink your name on the dotted line I'll send this out to every major bank and credit card company. Then they'll know that, despite your rebellious adolescence, you've calmed down and you're a safe bet. Also, as one of the perks, you'll be taken off every major airline's no fly list and be guaranteed safe passage through the borders of other nations at least nine times out of ten." He paused to let the magnitude of the offer sink in. Then he underscored it, saying "This is a very lucrative deal."

It could be fun, I thought. Having the toys everyone else had: a mortgage and a car, enough drugs to get me through the weekend. But I still had to say "No."

He didn't give me another chance. He placed the contract back into his briefcase. "Alright," he said. "Good luck to ya. I'm not going to let a little prick like you ruin my night. I've got a quota to fill." He took a straight razor from his briefcase and pulled it across my throat.

I woke with a start. I stared at the walls for a moment before I crawled out from under my duvet and went to the washroom. I flicked the light switch and looked in the mirror. There was no image in the glass staring back at me.

Being invisible has its moments, but we still haunt The Man's world and have to make a living here (if you can technically call it that). I've worked jobs where it mostly isn't a problem: night watchman, doughnut store monkey, that kind of thing. They're mostly jobs where they give me a uniform and none of the customers will ever look at my face and realize I don't have one.

One of the few times people can actually see me is when I'm drinking. First, I appear to be only a walking chalk outline, but the drunker I get the more I begin to flesh out. The process happens slowly over the course of the night. Far slower than a Polaroid picture developing, but not unlike it. You have to watch very closely to notice. Often you can find me and my friends looking blurry down at the bar, complaining about the world we abandoned in hushed tones. Our voices merge with the background music and chatter.

When we ghosts get lonely, the bottle is where we turn. It's great, you're not see-through anymore and can befriend the people from the world you left behind. There's still a buffer in place though. You can never tell them what you really think or what you really love, or else you will again become invisible to them. It's best to join in their discussions of television shows and recent purchases.

You can try to steer the conversation to your passions, but while you say "I've been having lots of sex in public washrooms lately," "I've been trying to write a book about how rainbows are sentient beings from another dimension," or "that fucking fucker Stephen Harper can suck my dick," they may nod but never reply. They smile, and for some of us that's enough.

Outside the bars we have our own community. We trade letters in the mail, which is a balm for the wear and tear induced by the daily grind. Mail carriers are half-ghosts themselves in these days of digital bullshit everything and they cast us sympathetic glances. We ghosts stay up late into the night talking to each other around kitchen tables and sleeping on each others' floors when we visit other cities. It's rarely comfortable, as we all live in terrible haunted houses. If we were visible we could ask for fewer mice roaming our apartments, hot water, or even storm windows (despite being incorporeal we still feel the winter cold).

The whole problem with being a ghost, though, is that the more you care about something the less tangible it becomes. It gets to the point where you start to wonder if it still exists. Doubt and depression are common among ghosts, they're the fall-out of our youthful anger. We all made a choice when we were younger that we sometimes regret now, with our empty bank accounts and rotting teeth, but we all come to accept that we are defined by it. As the song says, we "hum the satisfaction of progress / halted dead in its tracks."

We still march together when evil politicians come to town. We form a silent army that fills the streets of the financial district. We hold placards and smile at seeing so many other ghosts out, filling the streets with singing and chanting. Some go as far as renting cube vans and filling them with stereo equipment, turning them into pirate radio stations servicing the city block around them. But to all the regular people going about their day we just appear to be a layer of fog creeping across the city streets. A completely silent cloud rubbing itself against the sides of mirrored financial towers.

(Two Dollars Comes With Mixtape #5, 2005)

DINOSAUR PROVINCIAL PARK

HALFWAY BETWEEN REGINA AND DESPAIR MY DIRTY THUMB extended into the prairie sky. And that sky was too busy holding up the scorching July sun to pay any attention to me.

When I told Robbie of my plans to hitchhike across Canada, he nodded. "It's easy, just pick which way you want to go, right or left, then stick out your thumb." West of Winnipeg the mighty Trans Canada is reduced to a two-lane road.

That day, as the sweatband of my baseball cap got progressively blacker there was no traffic to be seen for miles. A prairie dog boldly sauntered across the two lanes of searing blacktop, reaching my side unscathed. I drank slowly from my water bottle. Canola and wheat stalks waved back and forth when a breeze came up.

The scale of this country is hard to imagine. Try this formula: Vast, times a million. So big it scared me when I was a child, clinging to the urban gridwork of Edmonton's streets and back alleys. The prairie sat just outside the city walls and I could feel it, just waiting for a chance to slip back in and sprout through the cracks in the sidewalks and holes in fences. Deer, foxes, and the occasional black bear patrolled the perimeter of the suburbs that buffeted the city from the tall grasses.

The first time I rode across the Prairies I was nine years old. My father had this habit, or rather this capacity, to drive heroic distances on our summer vacations. Eighteen hour stretches would melt away in a haze of exhaust and hourly news updates on the CBC. All he needed was a catnap here and there to refresh himself. Midday, in a rest stop, he would lower the minivan's beige bucket seat to nearly a forty-five degree angle, rest his aviators on the dashboard and drift off to sleep, his feet still firmly planted by the brake and gas pedals.

As my mother headed instinctively toward the johnny-on-the-spot, its blue plastic skin nearly disappearing in the cobalt Alberta sky, my brother and I wandered aimlessly down a farm access road. The gravel crunched under our sneakers and grasshoppers bounced off our tanned legs.

"There's so much space," I said, my bowl cut bobbing in the breeze.

My brother, four years older, nodded sagely, bringing my nascent thought to a higher plateau. "If the Prairies are this big, can you imagine how big space is? It's infinite!"

I pondered my brother's current obsession with outer space. This interest of his had already led to many sleepless nights for me, as most of our before-bed conversations concerned the logistics of certain reported alien abductions and sightings.

The road intersected a stretch of rail, and I hopped up on it. It led straight to the town's wooden grain elevator, emblazoned with the logo of the Alberta Wheat Pool, an iconic golden stalk.

Ten minutes later, my father was rested and content to drive the limit and be passed by everything on the road. I watched the odd cloud cast a shadow over the oceanic fields. Sure, we had CBC radio and spine-cracked Archie comics, but nothing could compete with the simple joy of watching the roadside passing. I sat in the backseat and the window's blue tint made me feel like I was in an aquarium, my head bouncing lightly against the rattling pane.

It was a ten hour drive south from Edmonton to Dinosaur

Provincial Park, but we had already stretched it to thirteen, with two more to go. It was the first of the twenty-one days of our camping trip, and we were just getting our sea legs. We had already acquired a small collection of oldies tapes, each purchased at a different gas station.

"Bad Bad Leroy Brown," "Down in the Boondocks," and "Devil with a Blue Dress On" was the soundtrack to the transformation of Alberta's geography from fertile plains into a spent desert. Rounded hoodoos cropped up beside the road, as smooth as bones.

In the sky, a premature night had taken hold and through the open window sudden cold weather raised goose bumps on my arm. That south Alberta sky shoots from the hip. There's nothing to obscure those white-fringed thunderheads that just build and build until the sky is ink and we bite our bottom lips anticipating the violence held in their bellies.

"Barometric pressure's falling," noted my father, the hobby meteorologist.

"Should we turn back?" asked my brother.

My father shook his head.

"Batten down the hatches," my mother said, pulling her slack seatbelt tight and rolling up her passenger side window.

I said nothing as we continued down the road, bracing ourselves for the coming storm.

(Ache #4, 2002)

2

TWO MEN

"TWO MEN LOST AT SEA, IN A LIFEBOAT," HE BEGAN TELLING HIS favourite joke, supporting himself on the thick arm of his recliner as he leaned in my direction.

"One says to the other 'What should we do?' So the other one sez 'Well it's looking pretty grim. I think we should do what we do in church.'"

Here he paused for effect. "So the other one took off his hat and passed it to him." He erupted in wheezy laughter.

"He passed the hat!" he repeated the punch line, still laughing.

I groaned and rustled the newspaper.

"Turn it up," he said, nodding toward the television, its volume already as high as it could go.

I lowered the paper long enough to watch a sports commentator deliver a brash opinion as statistics slid by beneath him. He stopped, and suddenly a red half ton truck was driving up the side of a mountain.

"All that crap," Lester said, waving his hand dismissively at the TV before looking out the window.

Lester slept in the dining room on an adjustable bed rented from the medical supply store. I slept upstairs, in my childhood bedroom. Since I was done high school but didn't yet have a job, I helped him those rare days that my mother had to leave the house.

"I think I gotta..." he said, a few minutes after the sports show had resumed.

I put down the paper and walked over to him. First I bent down and then, with his arms around my neck, slowly lifted him out of the blue easy chair. He leaned on me as we walked across the living room's dusty rug and into the kitchen, around the breakfast table and then into the small adjacent washroom. I always took care to support his left side, the one the stroke took. Placing him on the plastic booster seat he unfailingly thanked me for my gentleness.

Leaning on the kitchen counter I heard his farts resound like gunfire, the toilet bowl amplifying them. When I started helping him to the bathroom I remember being annoyed the first time I lifted him up and noticed that the toilet bowl was clear. "It was just gas," he told me, with no small amount of guilt in his voice.

After it happened again I began to sympathize, and fear the day that I too would be unable to distinguish between the need to shit and fart.

"Ready!" he called.

I opened the bathroom door and bowed. With his arms again around my neck, I slowly lifted him off the seat, pulling up his grey sweatpants in one swift tug. Leaning him against the counter I let the water warm before squirting liquid soap into his hands, waiting to lead him back to the living room.

The living room air was stuffy. For as long as I could remember my mother and grandmother had spent their afternoons here enumerating a census of family and friends who had fallen victim to a medical dictionary's worth of ailments, each one horribly distinct and distinctly horrible. Over tea and pink wafer cookies they sat where my grandfather and I sat now and discussed the details, the brass tacks of death. Some suffered on for years while others succumbed to the abyss in a moment.

One day I sat with them, bored and trying to watch *The Simpsons* on low volume, when my mother declared "In my sleep, with no pain! That's how I wanna go! Fast and easy!"

"Mom!"

"It's true! We've all gotta go sometime."

I rolled my eyes. No one I knew could ever actually die.

Lester was not immune to this obsession with mortality. After his stroke he read the obits every day, as he said, "to see that my name's not listed. Then I know I'm alive." But as the months and years of his depleted state dragged on he stopped making this habitual joke entirely—as if he had seen his name and was now debating whether or not to alert the authorities to their oversight.

"Let's go out," I said when I noticed the sun had broken through the March clouds.

"I don't know," he said. The television was still blaring, but instead he watched the movements of the backyard through the sliding door next to his La-Z-Boy. In the months since moving in he had observed the yard as it turned from grass to snow. Now it was both: a brown thatch and few stubborn patches of snow in the shadow of the cedars. "It'll be cold," he offered, as an excuse.

"C'mon."

"Alright," he sighed.

I wanted to open his life up to a little chance. Adventure. I got his purple bomber jacket, scarf and wool cap from the closet and wrapped him up. Then I opened the garage door and locked the wheels of the wheelchair and placed it outside the door. I put on his velcro outside shoes, grabbed a blanket for his legs, threw on my own jacket and shoes and hobbled him out the door.

"Easy now," he said as I pushed him down the incline of the driveway.

"Don't worry."

"Luba's car's gone," he said of the neighbour across the street. Lester began noticing things.

"She's probably volunteering at the museum today."

He nodded.

Up at the street corner a woman jogged past with a chocolate lab beside her. I watched his head turn, following them as they ran.

I took him out in the wheelchair when the weather was mild

and the roads clear. The suburb I grew up in was, for me, perhaps the least interesting place on the face of the Earth but still I wanted to make it sing for the old man. With every flower in a front garden, barking dog, piece of street refuse I tried to stir his own memory of all the flowers, dogs and garbage he had known. I tried to engage him in the drama of life outside, beyond the opera of his failing body.

A block away, the park was mud and unmelted snow, but the grey concrete paths were open. Children in snowsuits swung on the swing set while a mother watched indifferently from a bench.

I rolled the wheelchair next to a bench, locked the wheels, and sat down. When he was my age Lester was already working on the line of Ford's River Rouge plant in Detroit. That was at the beginning of his life, before he moved north to mine gold and years before he started a union, went on strike, was crushed and moved back to his hometown, which is my hometown, with his family. I knew that part, roughly. But what happened in Detroit?

"Not much. Worked. It was the biggest plant in the world," he said once when I asked him.

Today he remembered Shelly Brown, my former neighbour and childhood playmate.

"Did I ever tell you about Shelly?" he asked. I nodded, but he continued.

One year Lester was asked to dress up as Santa Claus and visit a class of second-grade students at the elementary school near his house.

"So I put on the costume and I'm a 'ho-ho-ho'in' and then I notice out of the corner of my eye, there's Shelly. But I think no, she can't recognize me in this outfit."

He smiled. "And then after I gave my little speech about being good and not asking for too much it's time for the kids to sit on Santa's lap and tell him what they want. And along comes Shelly, one of the last of them. And then she leans in real close and says 'Hello Santa,' and then whispers 'How's Nipper?'"

He laughed and laughed. Nipper was the little mutt that he followed around the neighbourhood for years.

I laughed, not with the childish glee I did the first time I heard the story many years before. But today it was actually kind of funny.

My grandfather wiped a tear of joy from his eye.

"Wasn't that smart? She knew it was me, but she didn't want to give me away."

(Negative Capability #1, 2008)

MERIDIAN PLACE

IT'S A LITTLE KNOWN FACT THAT I CAN MAKE MYSELF DISAPPEAR. I can slide through the thickest of crowds, climbing unnoticed over evening mall-shoppers and early morning dog-walkers. I can slip through the cracks in the sidewalks and surf a sewer tide. Returning to the surface, I emerge unharmed from the drain pipe, where the Norway rats have grown fat and long in the shadow of the old grain silo.

Mine was an insomniac childhood. In my safe suburban home I watched the ten o'clock news tell of nuclear arms buildups right before bedtime. As I tried in vain to find the path to slumberland, I wondered: would I be able to hear the bombs falling, or would the sky just light up?

To override my nuclear fears I turned on the lamp and read the picture books piled under my bed. I would begin with the book of Monsters (not scary), progress to the book of Ghosts (creepy) and then finally, I would read the book of UFO abductions (pretty damn frightening) with giddy terror. I let myself be scared to the point where sleep was impossible.

Those nights that I couldn't sleep I waited anxiously for my family to be unconscious before I crept down the stairs from my bedroom. I silently put on my sneakers, dragged the heavy front door closed behind me, and walked the streets. The night wrapped around my youth, and I studied it, observing its every angle. I kept busy by mowing the lawns of sleeping home-owners with a scythe. I joylessly performed BMX tricks in pyjamas on a moonlit dirt mound, while every other child in a seven kilometre radius was asleep.

Every night I crossed the paths of solitary cats. They weren't waiting for the end of the world like I was. Instead, they trusted their lives and the air in their lungs. As I walked I saw only the flashing eyes of calicos and tabbies who watched the night for signs of prey. After a hundred nights of walking, the cats came to the tips of driveways to greet me as I passed. I never gained their trust, but I did learn their tricks. They taught me to trust myself, to live free, avoid people, take what I need, worry less, and stick to the shadowy side of the street.

Even a decade later, I can assure you those skills gained from my sleepless childhood have been used to their fullest. The last three summers I worked a job where my only task was simply to stay up all night in a park. This night-watchman gig seemed to have been created specifically with me in mind. I already spent so many nights alone and awake from eleven until just past dawn that to get paid richly to do so seemed mildly ridiculous, like getting paid for breathing.

For the summer months, my corner of the park is stocked with theatre equipment valued in the tens of thousands of dollars. Large banks of lights hang from poorly erected scaffolds that, more than once, have fallen over in a wind storm. Collapsible wooden bleachers sit in front of the multi-level stage, which has been painted to look like the face of a giant walrus. The play began, I was told, with the actors emerging from behind a black curtain deep in the walrus' mouth and down a ramp painted to resemble a bright red tongue.

I was hired to sit in a wood-panelled Dickie Moore trailer, listen to CDs, read stacks of books, and make that corner of the park disappear. And while it couldn't be denied that I fulfilled my contractual obligations to a tee, I also left my post to skinny-dip with bathing beauties, had dirty sex on the trailer floor, and was smoked up by legions of thugged out teenagers who befriended me.

Occasionally I would look up from my book and watch the

temporary structures as they sat, still, waiting for the next day's performance of "Theatre Under the Stars" in all its blandness. The theatre world was, at its peak, one of debauched sodomites, sponsored by organized crime (not that du Maurier and Esso, whose grants to arts organizations fund my employers, are without blood on their hands), but now it has been whittled away to safe family entertainment. The poorly conceived renditions of seventeenth-century *commedia dell' arte* that are the company's bread and butter existed only to provide a substitution for the masses' powerful desire to see the circus.

The olde circus of freaks and barkers, tattoo tents and geek shows! Even the refined modern yuppies find a vacuum in their souls where the yearning for all things circus resides. Ashamed by the animalistic depths of their lust for the suspension of reality available only under the big top, they refuse to revel in the three rings. They retreat instead to the mild shits-and-giggles of that respectable institution known as theatre. Their hypocrisy disgusted me, yet their unhesitating payment of twenty dollars a head to spend an evening sitting in the park financed my weekly pay cheque. Thus, I was just another cog in that great machine of late twentieth-century 'entertainment,' which might as well have been labelled 'not the circus.'

Entertainment is clean and at a safe remove, but the circus is pure filth. There's rat shit behind the hot peanut seller and elephant shit in the box cars. Every kind of shit you can imagine is arrayed for your olfactory perusal, and it's all too close for comfort. Even when the big top is extinct we, the true believers, shall flock together. When moved by music, we will dance like organ grinder monkeys infested with ticks! We will lurk like whipped bears under the big top of the city! We will remember, like elephants, all the trespasses committed against us!

No thieves dared, or bothered, to trespass the holy soil of my tiny protectorate. Plenty of people came to visit though. Every so often I rolled up the steel shutters of the public bathrooms for a homeless couple who lived in the park. Most nights they preferred sleeping under the stars to the cold linoleum inside the park house. They came by only when the mosquitoes were swarming madly, driven to frenzy by a flashing electrical storm up-river.

Others came; third-shift workers for the Canadian Customs and Revenue Service, geniuses disguised in skin-tight bike messenger garb, and many friends fresh off cross-country trips. My trailer was often their first step back into society, after days of living within the suspended animation of Greyhound Bus Lines.

But now, the park stage was dismantled for another year, the company of actors disbanded, and the night-watchman sent on his way. That way was to a house-sitting favour for my parents, who were away camping for two weeks.

Skulking around in their basement at one in the afternoon, I surveyed my personal effects: a shelf of dollar paperbacks, two milk crates of LPs, and a monolithic grey filing cabinet. The rest of the concrete-floor basement was claimed by a century's worth of relics, exhumed and transported here upon the recent sale of my grandmother's home, five blocks away.

These objects defy inventory: shoe-boxes filled with memorabilia from my grandfather's days of organizing his fellow gold miners, others containing a wide assortment of Christmas cards received by my grandmother (Memere to her family, Jean to her friends) since 1974. On the couch sat a stereoscope and accompanying slides of an old Europe trip, and the Sears home barber kit which sheared me monthly until the age of ten.

All this paper and ephemera strewn about possessed the same value as the diamonds in the jewellery box on top of the Yamaha organ, or the mink coats in dry cleaning bags draped over the couch. My parents' basement storehouse was similar to a garage sale, where the 'thing-ness' of the items collected was plainly evident. The cultural and monetary values placed upon them had been stripped by the fact that they were now just unwanted objects. These relics from a sold home refused to disappear. Instead the mess crept across the basement, begging for some kind of order.

Intent on toasting some waffles, I emerged from the cool depths of the basement. But rather than stopping at the fridge, I continued through the living room, out the screen door, clear across the wooden rot of the deck, and down its wobbly stairs. Crossing the backyard I stopped halfway to the garden, and lay down in the grass. My parents' cat, the improbably named Squirrel, climbed onto my chest and sat there, refusing to move. Today, like most days, I got up at noon and forgot to feed this half-Siamese her breakfast of Eggs Benedict flavoured dried cat food.

Squirrel was raised by my old roommate, Jif. Jif's name, so similar to mine, caused so many crossed messages that many times I wonder if we didn't switch lives somewhere in the darkly comedic game of broken telephone our existence became. Jif loved Squirrel very much, and managed to imprint upon her a feline approximation of his uniquely bitchy yet lovable personality.

When Squirrel took sick, his dedication to her, and the protocols of cat ownership, was so complete that he had to give up his apartment, and even her company. He moved back to his allergic father's house to save money for her life-saving surgery. Somehow, after some impressive politicking on his part, *my* parents became caretakers of the cat that eventually drove Jif to bankruptcy. Even now, several months later, the scar from her surgery was still visible.

Light filtered through the eight-foot cedars bordering the yard on three sides. The sun was calming. It seemed to be patting me on the back.

"See, you're not doing so bad," the Sun said to me, startling me a little. "Sure, the last year mugged you, tear-gassed you, and broke your heart. But isn't it such a *nice* day?" The Sun, his voice not unlike that of James Earl Jones, winked at me over giant cartoon sunglasses.

"You're leaving soon, your pockets are full of cash from honest work..." There the Sun seemed to hesitate for a moment. That word, 'honest,' didn't ring true.

The Sun continued, delivering his coup de grace of cheeriness. "It's September and you don't have to go to school."

The Sun had me there. In the years since high school September had become my favourite month of the year. It's a cooler, more convivial August, one free from 'Back to School' type moping, so reminiscent of all those "I hate Sunday afternoon" conversations that punctuated our childhood.

"And look, there's not a cloud in the sky!"

I couldn't argue with the fiery sphere; things were looking up.

After filling Squirrel's bowl on the deck, I retired indoors to eat some of the bizarre processed foodstuffs my parents left in their fridge for me. All the food in their house was sheathed in seductive cardboard boxes emblazoned with bold logos. Over the course of my house-sitting term I studied these packages intently, trying to decide which food product was the least toxic. In the process, I developed a great affection for the design team at President's Choice, and devised ways in which I could headhunt one of them to design my fanzine.

Right, the fanzine, the whole reason I sent myself into this self-imposed suburban exile. I separated myself from my friends, who bathe in the bright lights of the city, so that I could avoid their company and other joys of life. The reason for this uncharacteristic hermitage was so I could put in the twelve hour days at my parents' dining room table required to proofread (poorly) then hand-letter the one hundred pages of my fanzine before I left town.

I talk about invisibility and disappearances, but to be honest, there is one place where my powers are useless, where I stick out like a sore thumb. It sits, three stories tall, on a suburban cul-de-sac named Meridian Place, a ten minute bike ride from my parents' house. There is no bike rack there, only a visitors' parking lot so optimistically large that the only day it ever approaches fifty per cent capacity is on Christmas Day. I lock my old ten speed to a thin sign post.

In my two weeks house-sitting, this was the only place I visited, and I did so every day. The building resembled the cookie cutter houses of suburbia, but while other suburban homes stopped growing at two stories, this one, painted a shade of blue-grey, stretched out to three, and took up nearly a full block.

I pushed the wheelchair access button and as the door mechanically swung open I immediately fell under suspicion. A massive grey-haired man in the atrium, skin hanging from his arms where muscles once were, called from an easy chair, "Hey loverboy, you here to see your girlfriend?" I said nothing in response, nor did I look the man in the eye as I crossed the carpeted lobby to the elevators.

The man yelled again, "I saw you kiss her," before the sluggish elevator doors closed.

"Mormons," my father explained upon my first visit here, two years ago. "They've built fifteen of these homes all across the States. This is the first one in Canada." He spoke with all the zeal of a franchisee getting in on the ground floor of a promising new chain of fast food restaurants.

"Do they use the same blueprints every time?" I said. "Like a goddamn Pizza Hut?"

My father nodded. "Not bad, eh? The model of efficiency. And look at this," he pointed to a framed print hanging on the wall, a French country home in autumn, rendered in pastels. "They spent over ten thousand dollars on art alone!" Along the wall, framed prints were placed at five foot intervals. The walls were decorated with whole orchards of fresh fruit rendered in still life, and folksy winter scenes, brimming with horse drawn sleds and rosy cheeks a-plenty.

As the elevator doors opened on the second floor, I saw Lucille sitting in an easy chair. Next to her hung more art, pictures of cherubic Victorian children sitting by a fireside. Lucille is a tiny woman. Standing four feet five inches tall, hunched over her walker, she appears almost fairy-like sitting down. A bald spot on the back of her snowy head reflected the hallway fluorescents.

"Oh Jeffrey," she greeted me in a deep Québécois accent, my name sounding closer to 'Jef-er-ray.' "Jean will be so glad to see you. It's so terrible. We're all upset. All those lives, people jumping from buildings holding hands..." News of disaster had arrived at the Crystal View Lodge long before it reached me.

My day began like any other. At two o'clock I called Memere to ask when I should come by to visit. Instead she told me to turn on the television, and now an hour later I was banging the brass knocker of her room, #207. A small label on the door beneath the brass knocker read R. Riopelle. A voice called from inside, and soon the door swung open. "Can you believe it?" she asked immediately. "Can you believe what they did?"

Memere, a half decade shy of being crowned centenarian, is what you might call 'old school.' Six months after her birth her parents emigrated from Le Pas, Quebec, first taking a train to the end of the northbound line, then packing a mule and whipping it twenty miles down a corduroy road. At the Frederickhouse River, the edge of the known world, they canoed thirty-five miles north and arrived in the northern Ontario settlement known as Camp Porcupine. It was little more than a mining outpost when her father opened the camp's first bakery, the White Star.

At the age of two, she and her mother rode their horse Nelly out into Lake Porcupine one day, until its legs were submerged. There they watched a bush fire claim every building in the settlement. Many drowned in the lake as late-comers, their skin on fire, surged forth, pushing the other waders out too deep. Unfortunate miners retreated underground on the advice of a foreman, and died in the mines as the fire sucked oxygen from the shafts. My great-grandmother sat out there for over twenty-four hours, wetting her daughter's hair and the horse's mane to protect them from the cinders swarming like mosquitoes.

When the fire subsided, all that was left of their home and bakery was the horse stable out back. Her father did not believe in insurance, as it interfered with the hand of God and His perfect plan for the world. And so poor old Nelly, the horse that saved Memere's life, lost her home. The stable was cleaned out, the floors scrubbed and the walls whitewashed, and the ungrateful Gervais family moved in.

"That was the North," Memere says nonchalantly, whenever the subject comes up.

I kissed her liver-spotted forehead and walked into the small beige room. Through her balcony window I saw a sky empty of clouds. People walked hurriedly along the sidewalk outside.

The television in front of the window played a continuous loop of videotape. A commercial airliner collided with one tower of the World Trade Centre, as the other was already in flames. Then the television showed the skyscrapers collapsing, one after the other, in a plume of dust and smoke.

"I bet those Muslims did it!" she intoned, disgusted. Her hair was white and her face deeply crevassed.

"Memere, it could be anyone, Muslims, Christians, atheists. It doesn't matter, whoever did it was crazy."

She nodded, not quite digesting my half-hearted message of inter-religious brotherhood. The truth was that war would follow, and that many people's belief in the very immediate reality of battle would supersede the more loosey-goosey 'turn the other cheek' ideals of their prophets.

We sat and watched the repeated fall of the North and South towers with the sound muted, reading occasional snippets of the headlines running across the bottom of the television screen. The day's events began to echo across the weeks, months and years to come. We sat still, in the room Memere's life had been collapsed into, until dusk collected in the corners of the room.

"Those poor souls," she said.

(Ghost Pine #7: Blood, 2003)

A MINER'S LIFE IS
LIKE A PILOT'S

IT'S ENGRAVED PERFECTLY ON MY MEMORY. WHEN I WAS FIVE MY grandfather and I would go flying around the neighbourhood in our ultra-light plane. He was always the pilot and I the passenger, but I'd still grab the steering wheel and hold it tight. We flew low, only forty feet over the neighbourhood, just above the tree-tops.

He'd call out our location: "Here's Canter Boulevard!" and point out my neighbours.

"There's Pat Badeen and Nick staking the grape vines in their garden!

"And there's Luba Brown pulling out of her driveway, off to work at the museum.

"And there's Zdena, Tom, and Dave Smetana swimming in their backyard pool."

True, our steering wheel was only the decorative circle carved in the back of an old chair in my grandparents' cluttered sun room and our plane was powered only by imagination, but to my five-year-old mind it was as vivid and real as the neighbourhood streets that tied us together.

And my Grampy was never a pilot but a miner by trade. He was also a shit disturber by nature. In 1953 he worked for the Brulan-Reef gold mine in Porcupine, Ontario, the only mine in town without a union. When Grampy organized a local of the C.I.O. and won a certification vote, the mine manager wouldn't acknowledge it.

This sparked off the long battle local media dubbed "the faceless strike," that lasted through the summer and into the dead of winter, ending when scabs came in, with the strike-pay drying up and the union broken. Grampy was blackballed out of town and came south with his family, initiating a long streak of stubbornness and leftist politics down the bloodline.

I lived just four blocks south of his house on Rita Avenue, so I saw him a lot. When he wasn't piloting me above the neighbourhood's skyline he was driving me up and down its tree-arched streets in his tiny blue Chevette. He'd take me to Robinson's Grocers or the pharmacy next door. He knew everyone; the produce aisle was filled with old acquaintances, the manager would stop to say hello on his way across the store and when he joked and flirted with the women at the drug counter I'd always ask "Doesn't Memere get jealous?" I was still oblivious to the fact that most women aren't attracted to 85-year-old men who have been married for well over half a century.

This shouldn't read like such a eulogy because I still see Grampy twice weekly if I'm in the city. Now he lives four blocks north of his old house, at the nursing home on Starwood. Only four blocks from his old home and he's still separated by an impassible gulf. Most times when I go see him I'll take him for a walk around the block in his wheelchair.

On our walks we tend not to stray too far. Up Starwood to Cordova where we stop in front of the flower shop. I sit on the grass and he tells me what he's been thinking about life and the neighbourhood. I try to tell him about the far-away cities I've been to, but those stories always fall flat due to unfamiliarity. So instead I fill him in on the small details about 114 Canter: familiar characters and a locale he knows like the back of his calloused miner's hands.

We talk, but silence inevitably falls and an awkward one too, since we're both thinking the same thing: that somewhere between the two minor strokes on the right side of his brain, and my inelegant survival of adolescence, our roles have been reversed. The pilot has become the passenger.

(Otaku #5, 1999)

3

PUNK ROCK IS OUR LIVES

A FEW WEEKS AGO I MANAGED TO GET OFF WORK EARLY AND made my way down to the Vincent Massey park bandshell to catch the punk prom. I was in my dressy work clothes but everyone I spoke to in dirty old clothes had bigger ambitions than mine.

Everyone was there, kids I've known since pre-school dancing next to kids I met last week. We danced around each other so elegantly to the scratchy sounds of mix tapes we'd played to death on the shitty ghetto blaster when we all ate lunch together in front of my locker.

When the sun went down we pulled in close to witness the main attraction. The headlining band was full of high school comrades; after years of playing seven nights in a row at punk clubs and art galleries all over town they finally pooled enough cash to put out their first record. The funny thing is I never saw them at any of the shows that were talked about later, I only saw them play in the strangest places.

The Christmas assembly where they wore suits but still ended up clearing the cafeteria, the barbecue at the school down the street where Nick cussed out the principal and I beamed, so proud. Punk rock not at the club but punk rock in the pre-school. In the basement, at the park and on the roof of the mall.

I was even at their first show. Hell, I put it on. For the school's annual Band Warz somebody thought it would be a good idea to set up a small second stage in the big foyer and put me in charge of it. The result was a mosh pit by the vending machines and skanking by the recycling bins. It was a near-riot when the organizers cut our power because we were making too much noise and diverting attention from the main spectacle, jumbo TV, dry ice and all.

When they played their second set, playing the same songs over, their drummer's blister broke and blood flew all over the borrowed drum kit. Alan never cleaned it off, since it was the most punk rock thing we'd ever seen. The whole thing was a bloody mess but with that debut they had no option but to succeed, or flunk out of high school trying.

So when I say we pulled in close to watch them I mean really close. Smiling at each other as every familiar drum fill, guitar squeal and bass line brought back memories of growing up and the tough times music got us through. Smiling at the high pitched screams and the words that went with them, they'd turned into anthems over the years.

Shitty mix tapes and even worse ghetto blasters, bad plans and even worse outcomes, our defiance and camaraderie meant the difference between punk and the rest of the world. We pulled together close, grinning, even if we hadn't made it all the way we'd made it far enough to put on our own prom, write the songs to go with it and the sappy stories that follow. That's good enough, let's forget the casualties tonight.

We pulled even closer when the lighting storm hit. All of us hiding out under the band shell, watching the band and the accompanying light show of sparks flying from the damp amps. In between songs Alex laughed: "It's punk against the elements!" I laughed too because I know that's a battle we'll win every time; it's the battle of punk against time that we may have already lost.

(Otaku #4, 1999)

RECORD REVIEW
Union of Uranus *To This Bearer of Truth* (Feral Ward, 2004)

IN 1994 MY FRIEND SARAH WAS IN GRADE EIGHT AT Glashan Intermediate School, between the highway and the bus station in downtown Ottawa. Sometimes toward the end of the school year, when the windows were open, she could hear a muffled booming from down the street. It sounded like a pile driver (except she didn't know what a pile driver was yet) and it started and stopped all through Math class.

On lunch break she walked down Arlington to buy french fries from Ada's Diner. On the way she passed a pack of feral boys sprawled all over the street in front of the old TV repair shop. They were older, maybe even done high school, but acted like stupid kids, doing skateboard tricks and playing chicken with the cars turning off Bank Street.

Sarah averted her eyes as she passed them, and walking back to school she noticed the boys had retreated into their house? or store? or clubhouse? and the heavy pounding had begun again.

Ten years later Jon sent me a copy of all his old band's songs collected on one CD. When I listened to it I didn't think of how rad or seminal they were or how many times I had listened to that split seven inch with Immoral Squad. All I remembered were my toes freezing in my boots a few days after New Year's 1996 at 5 Arlington's last show.

The heat had been cut and the lease was over and all the bodies pressed together couldn't make enough warmth to compensate. (I think the electricity was cut too because there was only a lamp on in the corner, but then how were the amps so fucking on?) Stomping my feet I was just one of a hundred at the show waiting to hear them play "Believer" right after they had already started it and fucked it up twice.

(Ghost Pine #9: Bees, 2005)

WOULD CODE NAMES BE ASSIGNED?

"THIS IS LIKE TOTAL CENSORSHIP. I CAN'T BELIEVE THIS LAW IS going to go through!" I said as I leafed through the paper's City section.

Cat nodded in agreement. Then she said "Shut up and kiss me."

Down at city hall there was a by-law on the table banning postering on telephone poles and street lamps. Posters were my lifeblood; on my weekly trip downtown I stopped dozens of times to decipher the new batch. I took offence at City Hall trying to stop one of the truly public art forms, and stifling one of the few attempts punks made at communicating with the outside world.

Tempers flared as word of the pending by-law spread. Shawn set a date for the resistance to meet and devise a strategy, Friday night at midnight. Cat and I took up the challenge. A propaganda counter-attack. Together we copied a hundred copies of our vaguely threatening poster, which read "We will not be silenced!" in big bold letters. On the appointed night I found my way to Shawn's house, beneath the Queensway. As I rang the bell I wondered if there would be a password in effect.

Shawn let me in and I took a seat on one of the living room couches. A quick glance around the room revealed a motley crew, gathered from every corner of the city. We had each cut and pasted hundreds of anti-by-law flyers, getting our message across with varying degrees of menace.

A dirty dozen freedom fighters, we were prepared to defend our cause, to the death if necessary. Everyone wore black from head to toe, myself included. We were clandestine as fuck, and eyed each other suspiciously. Would code names be assigned?

"Well, I guess everyone's here." Shawn broke the silence at quarter past.

"So what's the plan?" I asked. Tonight there was no wall we wouldn't scale, no lock we wouldn't pick, no member of city council we wouldn't assassinate in cold blood. Shawn need only say the word and set us loose.

"Uh, shit, what do you guys wanna do? I just thought we could put some posters up around town." This plan wasn't nearly as treasonous as we had hoped.

Near the door a kid in a black leather jacket with a tuft of fiery red hair spoke up. "I know where the mayor lives. Why don't we go poster her street, man?"

His name was JB, a tactical genius in our war of wheat paste and righteousness. Our army stayed out all night, wallpapering the mayor's suburban street with our bold opinions, staining our black clothes with gummy white paste.

Of course the by-law passed unanimously. Perhaps our protest contributed to its speedy ratification. The law states that a poster can only be put up twenty-one days or less before a show and must be pulled down twenty-four hours after it takes place. Most posters fall victim to the winter wind and spring sleet before the city employees can get to them.

"I wish I was still as angry as I was when I was fifteen," said JB, four years later in Montreal. He was the first to break the silence that had already followed us out of the movie theatre and down the block. Seeing the old Dead Kennedys stencil at the corner of Milton and Hutchinson forced him to speak.

"JB, if any of us were as angry as we were when we were fifteen, we'd be dead." said MP.

"Or in jail," I added.

All month long the movie theatre was showing punk movies every Friday at midnight. It was in a crummy little theatre but if the film was delayed they would play a scratchy mixtape from 1985 over the stereo. In the rows some dressed in spikes and chains while others wore Brooks Brothers. In the booth the projectionist cued up the ancient print.

The movies made us laugh and groan. A cherubic Billy Idol sang "Kiss Me Deadly" as his bleach blonde liberty hawk flopped to and fro. Nancy tried to fuck Sid on camera, but Vicious passed out in the middle of doing the deed. But there were also moments when time stood still, or cracked wide open. Poly Styrene danced in circles screaming "Bind me, tie me, chain me to the wall / I want to be a slave to you all!"

Tonight's flick had none of those blinding moments. It was a documentary about a tribe of Hollywood gutter punks who survived by wits alone. The film, after two hours of misery, ended on an almost hopeful note, until an epilogue revealed that two of the punks later died when their squat caught fire. After that the other punks all vanished from the streets, gone and forgotten.

"When I was fifteen," JB continued, putting his collar up against the wind, "I worked at a video store near my mom's house. All my friends abandoned me when they discovered booze and cigarettes. I walked around wearing a big trench coat I stole from my dad, wondering 'Is this all there is to life: loneliness and recurring nightmares of nuclear holocaust?'

"Then I found the Dead Kennedys, their music was written for me only, I swear. I still dreamt of the end of the world but it sorta became a joke. Instead of being depressed I hated everything. But I could laugh at it too!"

I was impressed by his nostalgia. And who doesn't long for the days when the world was so simple that every turn of the newspaper page revealed another symptom of the world's surely terminal disease? JB at fifteen had a true rage, as apocalyptic as it was adolescent.

We met every other night at a café near the children's hospital. Loud dance music blew out of the stereo, competing for our attention with music videos flickering across a big-screen TV. I watched JB and MP dote on each other, kissing each others' cheeks and hands. It was embarrassing.

MP went home at two a.m. and then JB and I walked the streets telling stories. One night we walked the sidewalk of a four-lane street in the financial district. Vacant skyscrapers stood all around us. On several floors the lights were left on for the cleaning staff. The street was completely empty and I realized I'd never seen it in the light of day. I had no idea what the people who worked in those buildings looked like.

"I love this town, but some nights I feel like it could swallow me whole," I admitted. "I could just disappear and no one would miss me."

"That's not true. I'd miss you a hell of a lot," said JB without skipping a beat. Maybe all that hate in his black leather heart turned to love somewhere between home and here, then and now.

(Ghost Pine #6, 2001)

MIXTAPE REVIEW
"Some Music for J." (By Andy, 2003)

"LISTEN, DO YOU KNOW ABOUT REMBETIKA MUSIC?" SAID Andy after the morning's first espresso. His one-year-old, Sam, born in the very living room we sat in, crawled the floor playing with wheeled wooden toys shaped like trucks, ducks and rainbows.

Bill the pitbull walked up to me holding her slobber-coated kong. The muscles in her neck grew taut as I struggled to pull it from her until she pitied me enough to loosen her grip. I threw the toy and it soared through the room. Bill ran after it, taking care to avoid the blonde child in her path.

"Check this out," Andy said with excitement, a change from his usual hardened demeanor. "At the end of the First World War, there were these Greeks. They were living in Turkey, but they had to flee because uh, the Ottoman empire, yeah I think that's right... protected 'em, but now the Turks wanted to wipe 'em out, eh? Even though, y'know, they'd been living there a while."

Sam crawled over to the stand where Andy's bass sat, grabbing at the instrument with tiny hands.

"Ah, that's daddy's bread and butter," he said to his son. Striding across the room, Andy grabbed the bass, sat and began playing licks for the boy's enjoyment.

"So these exiles ended up in Athens. Totally fucking unemployed cuz there's this post war depression shit. And so they

just hung out in the cafés, smoking a lot of hash and inventing
this music some call the Greek Blues. It's all these crazy-ass
songs. The songs are about their old homes and being broke
and high, all that good shit. That's what I've been told, but I
don't know a fucking word of Greek."

He laid the bass on the couch and produced a cassette from
the breast pocket of his plaid shirt. After turning on the stereo
and waiting a second for it to hum to life he put in the tape and
pressed play.

The tape hissed before the first chords scraped out of time
and into the air around us. The music was spare and weird
sounding, jangly instruments with howling vocals that were
both there and not. I don't know Greek either but the singer
sure sounded fucked up about something.

"More coffee!" Andy scooped up Sam from the couch and
handed him to me before rolling back into the kitchen. I
received the weight of the child awkwardly but briefly managed to bounce him on my knee in time to the music. Next
he climbed off my knee, onto the couch and down from the
couch, landed on his diapered behind and started crying.

"What the hell'd you do to the boy?!" Andy yelled from
the kitchen where he was shovelling grains into the stovetop
espresso maker.

A year later Andy sent me a tape with some of the songs he
played for me that morning in Vancouver. The ghost voices
ululated in my headphones as I walked my hometown streets
on Christmas Eve to meet Chris at the Merivale Road Denny's.

The rain came down lightly, spitting and covering my glasses in a thin film that blurred all the Christmas lights hanging
from eaves and front-lawn trees into a refracted halo of sparkling. It felt like the whole world was cracked and its spirit was
leaking away, which is how I often feel when I walk in the rain
after drinking a few beers.

(Ghost Pine #9: Bees, 2005)

BOOK REVIEW
Get in the Van by Henry Rollins (2.13.61, 1994)

I used to work in my grandmother's garden. Her eyes distinguished flower from weed far across the lawn even when they were to me the same shape and shade of green. She had no notebook or map, she just remembered where she planted everything.

I often searched the tin shed for twine or scissors or the axe. Shelves held rusted garden tools and gloves with holes and smaller things forgotten in one-pint strawberry cartons, their sides reading "Ontario Fruit."

At the time I was reading *Get in the Van* by Henry Rollins in my off hours. As a result every time I was in the tiny backyard structure I was inspired to ask my grandparents if I cleaned it out would they let me sleep in it for the summer.

Rollins's book of tour diaries was boring except for the entries written in the shed he lived in behind Greg Ginn's mother's house. In the shed he wrote about being broke in a city obsessed with money, passive-aggressive band members, the letters he got from his pen-pals Nick Cave and Diamanda Galas and the cops that harassed him on his walk to the 7-11.

For some reason all that shit seemed so glamourous to me that summer. Looking back now it's hard to understand why. After eight years of being broke, dealing with passive-aggressive friends and being harassed by cops (I can't complain about the pen-pals) I wonder if I should have been reading another book instead.

Each time I left the shed I wondered if I should ask them, then forgot. Emerging into the sunlight I tied swathes of weeds with twine, threw them into the yellow wheelbarrow and rolled everything to the garbage pile on the curb.

I've yet to live in a shed.

(Ghost Pine #9: Bees, 2005)

4

WINNIPEG

I'D ALREADY BEEN ON THE BUS FOR THIRTY-SIX HOURS WHEN IT pulled into Winnipeg. And since Stefanie always said her town was utopia I thought I'd give it a shot.

I walked around the corner from the station and found the library waiting for me. When I was growing up and other kids were playing softball, BMX, and doctor, smoking behind the shed, I was at the library. Looking at art books and reading bad young adult novels in the basement, growing up among the stacks.

I found a map and searched for the posh Anarchist bookstore I'd been to once before, with stone walls, high ceilings and good-looking staff. I hung out there probably longer than I should have, succumbing to my bad habit of sticking around just to hear familiar songs on the tape-deck. I sang along under my breath.

I picked up that habit in some Calgary coffee joint where I wrote a letter to my grandfather and made eyes at the counter girl for refills, even though she'd always wink and say "These aren't usually free..." All just to kill time until the record ended. Sorry Gramps.

I walked around town and wondered what it was all about. I watched the people on the street and wondered why I couldn't run into any of those brilliant, good looking peace punks whose records I'd listened to, zines I'd read and photos I'd seen over the years.

Where were all those kids Robbie told me stories about?

Where were my old pen pals? And why was everyone asking me for directions? Couldn't they see I was as confused by the crooked streets as they were?

It had already been a long road home. After hours of watching prairie towns roll by I was finally lost in one. Now I know why country songs are written.

I was cultivating a bad mood so I headed down to the bridge to do the clichéd punk thing and skulk. I wrote my name on a wall and walked across the cracked dry mud to the river bank. It wasn't until my jeans were covered in mud up to my knees that I realized it wasn't so dry after all. I crawled out of that quicksand more animal than man.

I walked down to the bank, took off my pants and rinsed them out in the muddy river. I wished I knew some of those old spirituals to sing. The ones that seem to be about washing but are really coded messages and mythologies.

As it was I just knew a Waylon Jennings song. The one about babies, outlaws, ladies, bankers and even a bunch of stray dogs. What a great song. I rinsed it all out in the muddy Assiniboine. Winnipeg's supposed to be the friendliest city in Canada but of all the boats that motored past only one slowed down and they just laughed at me. Fuckers. Well, I was laughing too, but still...

The late August sun hid behind the clouds and the jeans weren't drying. I put them on and watched the train go by, one of those long prairie freights. I found a coin wash and stood around in my boxers and the old lady that ran the place laughed when I told her my sad-sack story.

With dry pants the town didn't seem so bad. Two girls on the street sold me some lemonade in a plastic beaker, I found the cheap Ethiopian restaurant that takes forever to serve, and young lovers smiled at me sympathetically, lit up by the Christmas lights on the trees by the legislature.

I walked back to the station and late summer night pulled in. It was that darkest prairie night that used to scare me so much as a kid; I always thought I could see monsters in it.

It was time to disappear all over again, but I guess it isn't disappearing when there's no one around to notice I'd gone.

I pulled out the muddy map of America I'd kept in my back pocket all trip. As the door of the prairie closed behind me I fell asleep and my dreams traced the road home: from the 'Peg to the Sault, Thunder Bay, North Bay, Ottawa. And the credits rolled on summer.

(Otaku #4, 1999)

ON TRUANCY

"IT WAS A SUMMER JOB. ONE OF DAD'S FRIENDS WORKED FOR the Ministry of Transportation, and he put in a good word for me. We left in June on the Cornwallis. It was an ice breaker that sailed out of the port of Montreal, and we made our way down the St. Lawrence.

"Eventually we sailed along the Labrador coast, stopping in all the communities along the way, unloading for a day or two and then sailing to the next community. We had to unload these huge barrels of supplies, and bags of coal, and take them up to the high water mark, so they wouldn't be submerged when the spring thaw melted the ice.

"We worked in eight-hour shifts. There were only six of us student workers along with the regular crew. We waited their tables in the mess hall, four meals a day, and unloaded the supplies.

"It was summer, and the sun never set. The Eskimos never went to sleep, they used to sing and dance all night, it was really something to see. Some days we would see the northern lights in the afternoon.

"The only thing I could never get used to was the smell of oil from the engine room, it was so acrid, and you could smell it through the whole ship. And some days as we got further north I would wake up to hear this loud grinding sound, it was the ice butting against the hull, I could hear it in my bunk.

"The second year I went up on the C.D. Howe, that was '56 and they were setting up the DEW line: distant early warning. There was so much to do, they were setting up radar centres in the high North, so they could detect any missiles coming over the pole from the Soviet Union. We delivered to the one at Fox Basin.

By the second week of September we'd made it to Coral Harbour, on Southampton Island in Hudson Bay, almost at the Arctic circle. I'd already missed a week of high school when I learned that the ship wasn't going back south. Because of all the DEW deliveries it was behind schedule, the regular crew had to finish the deliveries before the ice got thick in October.

"One of the other student workers was a little older, and he was a student at the U of T. He was anxious to get back to his studies, and the city. Coral Harbour had a little landing strip, so we figured we'd hitchhike together."

"You hitchhiked *planes?* How old were you?" I asked my father.

"Oh, I must have been... sixteen or seventeen. We caught a DC 3, and it flew us all the way over Hudson Bay to Churchill, where we stayed the night in some army barracks. The next day we begged our way onto a flight to Detroit. I can't remember how we got it or what kind of plane it was, but it was a long flight.

"From Detroit I figured we were close enough to get a bus, but this University guy was determined and he talked up some pilots at the airport and landed us a flight on a private jet, a Lodestar, owned by the executive of the Massey Ferguson tractor company, which, for some reason, was flying without passengers back to Toronto.

"That night I stayed at the Y. The next morning I got up, grabbed a cup of coffee and walked down to the Greyhound station and got a bus to Ottawa. I remember that ride well, it was September and the leaves had just changed and they were beautiful, shades of orange, yellow and red like fire. I stared out the window the whole way home. The next day I was back in high school."

(Ghost Pine #7: Blood, 2003)

JET FUEL

THIS IS THE HARD PART TO EXPLAIN ABOUT HITCHHIKING: THE slow death of waiting. It seems endless since there is no distraction from the steady stream of big rigs and cars rolling by. It's always the same: some people will smile sympathetically, others make indecipherable hand signals, still others sneer, but most just ignored us and drove on by.

After hours of waiting someone finally picked us up and drove us to the furthest reaches of Toronto's eastern suburbs. He had been a hitchhiker himself, once, and as he dropped us off he told us he was sure we'd have no trouble getting a ride across to the other side of Toronto, which was easy for him to say as he peeled off in his new car.

Luckily for him, he was right, so I didn't have to put a curse on him and his children and his children's children, etc. We got a ride all the way across Toronto to St. Catharines, easy. On the way our driver pointed at an overpass down the road. "See that bridge?" We both nodded.

"Well, when that bridge was first bein' built, 'round about ten years ago, my friend Chuck had a little run-in with it while he was, y'know, a li'l bit DUI." He made the drinky-drinky motion with his hand and we wondered what he was getting at.

"You see, Chuck used to haul freight, not no milk or cookies, nothing like that. See, Chuck hauled jet fuel.

"He bailed out at the last minute all right, but that there overpass got blown to kingdom come. Chuck, he don't haul freight no more."

He dropped us off in St. Catharines right at a truck stop. Perfect. The sun was setting fast, but a lonely trucker was sure to pick us up. In fact, we were so sure that we let the last few minutes of daylight slip away and got two plates of fries from the truck stop diner. After a day of standing on the side of the highway inhaling emissions, there's no limit to the amount of good to your spirit a plate of food can do. Even pseudo-food like fries.

But back on the highway the once-bright spring sun sunk faster than we'd anticipated and our chances for a ride sunk with it. All the truckers looked at us like we were from Mars and our on-ramp spot was terrible, under construction and without enough of a shoulder for a tricycle to pick us up, much less an eighteen wheeler. The night, and our spirits, went black.

My mind flashed back to Jon Sharron's few words of advice to me when I started hitching. "First, no woman on her own is ever going to pick you up, and if the sun goes down, shit, you might as well be holding a bloody axe."

But before worry could lead to hyperventilation a tiny red coupe pulled over: saved! And as I got in I saw it was driven by a woman. What a stroke of luck, both Sharronist hitching rules broken at once. I made a mental note that I instantly forgot to start playing the lotto. True, she could only take us a few miles, but anything was better than the on-ramp death I'd envisioned.

A half hour and back to the highway. It was even later and darker than before and an O.P.P. cop kicked us off the 401, leaving our only option a tiny gas-station in the middle of no-where, but before I had a chance to look for a ditch to sleep in we got a ride from Mark, heading straight to Windsor, across the lake from the Motor City.

Of all the long-winded rides I've had, Mark was by far the worst, spending hours giving me the run down of his job and the economics of his industry all in impenetrable jargon. It took me two hours to figure out that he looks at radar pictures of rocks to see if there are precious metals in them. Yawn. But as we made our final approach on Windsor we started talking about politics and constructed a caffeinated / no sleep thirteen-point program to destroy the government. I'm continually surprised at how many drivers have told me "I'm no anarchist, but the government should be overthrown by force!" It gives me hope.

He dropped us in Windsor and he was our last hitch so this is where the story ends. But, for the record, it took us another twelve hours to travel the final twenty miles: to get into Detroit, get lost downtown, catch a shuttle bus to the airport, and walk the last miles on foot, alongside the highway. Then, when we finally got to the hall where the show was, no one was there, it was ten a.m. We pulled off our shoes and socks and after over twenty-four hours and nearly a thousand kilometres covered we finally fell asleep, on the front lawn.

(Otaku #5, 1999)

ROCKO

"SO HOW'S YOUR LITTLE BOY?" ASKED THE WOMAN IN THE PINK sweater sitting at the diner counter next to me. Her question was addressed to the enormous woman sitting on the stool behind the restaurant's cash register.

"He's breakin' my heart. He called me last night to tell me that he can't make it up this weekend. You know, he goes to that school down state."

The woman next to me offered a few excuses in the absent son's defence. "Maybe he's got a girlfriend down there," she laughed.

"Nah, it ain't that," said the disappointed mother. "He says he's got to study. He's going away to do a semester in Italy next month. This was the only weekend he could make it home before leaving." The woman at the cash was the matriarch of this breakfast joint and was constantly engaged in tiny conversations with her patrons.

"Seems like just yesterday I was bouncin' him on my knee," the pink sweater lady said as she paid her bill, dropping three quarters into the tip jar.

"Uh-huh. You be safe now."

"I'll see you tomorrow, Rosalita."

Rosalita turned to me and smiled, as if forgetting her woes, and asked "And what can I get for you, baby boy?"

I sat at the counter of the Cozy Corner diner almost every morning that I was in Chicago. Over coffee and pancakes I read the *Tribune*'s headlines of the 'inevitable war' that was waiting somewhere, offstage.

It was still September, and from my vantage point on the Greyhound bus that I rode from Toronto to Chicago, it seemed that every billboard in this country bore the message "God Bless America." The same slogan could be found on t-shirts and knick-knacks in the dollar stores of Milwaukee Avenue. Every window in the city was covered in the Stars and Stripes. Small flags were even sold on highway off-ramps by gang-bangers wearing corn rows and capped teeth. The Cozy Corner was no different. Pulled from the daily papers, the newsprint flags taped up in its windows were beginning to yellow in the strong autumn sun.

A block away from the Cozy Corner was the apartment of one of my oldest friends, Michelle. When I met her in my hometown, she was a nomadic punk who kept forks and knives on her wallet chain and told me she didn't wear any clothes that she couldn't wipe her hands on.

I have a whole drawer in my filing cabinet of letters Michelle has sent me over the years. They chart the end of her nomadic days, her enrolment in university, roommate woes, the plethora of shitty jobs she worked to support herself, activism, graduation, and finally the beginning of her career as a teacher at an alternative high school.

When I arrived in the city a few days earlier, she was at work. When I called, I got her roommate McKay on the line, who gave me directions from the bus station. "I'm just working on some art with a friend," she said into the crackly pay phone. "Come on over."

I walked a short block from the El train and then up the stairs of her building and rang the bell. McKay came down the stairs to let me in and gave me a big hug. Her short spiky hair was bleached, and big patches of whiskers graced either side of her chin. There were paint stains on her white tank top.

"Come on in. Me and a friend are working on a project on the back porch." McKay was a graduate of the School of the Art Institute of Chicago, the most prestigious art school on the continent.

I followed her upstairs and through the long apartment to the back deck where, rather than a styled-up design student, I found McKay's partner in art was a six-year-old boy.

"Alex, this is Jeff." McKay introduced me, picking up one of the tubes of paint off the floor of the deck and mixing it with water in an empty yoghurt container.

"Hi," I said.

He said "Hi" back as he attentively painted an empty cereal box black. Next to him, tied to the railing, was a Chihuahua with bulging eyes.

"This is my dog, Rocko," said Alex proudly. Rocko made a nervous sound. I couldn't tell if he was sneezing or barking as I pet his twitchy head.

"Jeff's from Canada," McKay said.

"When's the last time you were there?" Alex asked, putting down his brush and fidgeting with his dollar sign necklace.

"I was just there this morning."

Alex perked up. "I love it there! I went last December when I was five-and-a-half. There were palm trees and I swam in the ocean!"

"In Canada? Really?"

"Oh. No," he said absentmindedly, "in Puerto Rico. That's where my parents are from." In his binary six-year-old mind there were only two places in the world: Chicago and Puerto Rico.

Alex immediately switched gears. "This," he showed me his cereal box, "is a building in my city!"

"It's a project for school," McKay clarified, as she painted white windows on an already green-coated Pringles tube.

"It's going to be so COOL!" Alex screamed, as only a child can.

"You behavin' up there?" Alex's mom instantly appeared on the balcony below. Her stern look turned to a smile when she spoke to McKay. "If he's actin' up don't hesitate to send him down here."

"I won't," McKay smiled.

"Painting my city, painting my city," Alex sang. Rocko provided accompaniment, barking in time as his owner put grey stripes of windows across his miniature office tower.

That night, after we ate grilled cheese sandwiches, Michelle took me across town on the El train. In this plains city, riding the train at six p.m. provided the best view of the sunset in the West. Michelle missed it though. As soon as we sat down on the train she fell promptly asleep on my shoulder. Worn out from her first year as a full-time teacher, she had a habit of falling into instant slumber on the rickety trains. She woke up a half-minute before it pulled into our stop, her sleeping mind still counting off stations.

Getting off the train we crossed one of Chicago's many seven-street intersections, which Michelle told me were paved over old Native pathways. We went in the front door of a café and down a flight of stairs to the basement. At the far end of the concrete room was a stage, only a foot or so high. In front were rows of seats like those found in run-down cinemas.

"Would you like to read tonight?" a tall teenager dressed from head to toe in street wear asked, holding an expectant clipboard.

"Gawd, you're like the third person to ask us," Michelle laughed. "We're just here to watch tonight, sweetie," she said and the kid blushed and fled.

Sitting in our high-backed chairs, I couldn't gauge what we were in for. Hip-hop high schoolers milled about, laughing and socializing awkwardly in clusters around the room.

"These kids are part of the Young Chicago Authors program," Michelle whispered in my ear. "They join up in the ninth grade and if they stick with it all the way through high school, going to weekly meetings and doing these readings, they get scholarships for college."

"Alright, it looks like I'm the MC this fine evening." The lanky kid had abandoned his clipboard for a microphone, clearly relishing his moment in the spotlight. "As you all know, my name is Dave, but I MC under Immaculate." He let his chosen name sound out for a second and one of his boys cheered from the audience, while others straight up laughed. "You'll be hearin' my skills a little later on, but first up here on stage tonight we have..." he consulted the clipboard, "Shelagh! Come on girl, get on up here and show us what you can do!"

Over the next two hours an equal number of boy and girl poets graced the stage. The boys tended to spit rhymes about lofty political issues and speak too fast in newfound deep voices. They were one part Dan Rather delivering the nightly news, and another part KRS ONE, taking it personally. The girls slowed it down, lyricizing about all things tender, speaking in sultry deep voices about their new bodies and the boys they let touch them.

Cutting across the gender divide was one universal subject. Every single poet had a verse about the El train in their repertoire. It made sense. As teenagers one of the cheapest tastes of freedom is riding mass transit clear across the city, whether going to your girlfriend's house at midnight, to play ball in the park, or just nowhere.

For the first thirty seconds they were on stage, the readers talked fast, stumbling on their words and apologizing. But a minute into delivering a poem they would become fully submerged in the world they'd built on the page. When their poem ended abruptly they slowly awoke from the trance, wishing they hadn't run out of words.

The younger brother of one of the teen poets, a seven-year-old named Martin, read his first poem. "Snow," he spoke in total monotone. "Snow/ in December: snow/ covering the world/ piles like mountains/ cold like ice/ Snow."

Finally, the Master of Ceremonies returned to the stage as promised, in the guise of microphone-controller Immaculate.

"I know y'all is tired, ya butt cheeks are hurting, but right about now I'm going to play a little freestyle game with ya. To prove just how dope an MC Immaculate be, when I make this signal," he lifted his right hand and spread his fingers, "I want y'all to shout out a word, any old word, and I'll fit it into my rhyme routine. Feel me?"

The audience immediately began screaming out words and Immaculate deftly juggled *pancreas*, *erectile*, and *anthrax* among others. But at the two minute mark his rhyme scheme fell apart. He was greeted, as were all his peers that night, regardless of talent, with a unanimous wall of hands clapping and mouths screaming praise.

On my last day in Chicago I wanted to see the city from the Sears Tower sky deck, but it was closed until further notice in the fear of terrorism. Instead I spent the day lost in the Chicago Loop. I was looking for the library half-heartedly, trying to remember what corner it was on without bothering to consult a map or even ask anyone where it was. Instead I wandered in the rain, getting soaked while staring at the stumpy gothic buildings and the stark towers that crowded the skyline.

The rain eventually escalated to the point where the phrase "cats and dogs" became appropriate. The fiery trees of autumn were slowly being stripped bare and their orange and yellow leaves clogged the storm drains.

Along the streets of department stores, Hallowe'en decorations already crowding their window displays, I found a mall carved into the husk of an old high-rise. I pushed open the heavy brass doors and was glad for the shelter. My shoes, heavy with rain, slapped against the marble floor. I followed signs that read "Food Court" with arrows pointing straight up. I rode the escalators past all the boutiques until I arrived on the eighth floor.

The food court was housed in a yawning atrium where a few fast food outlets lined either wall. The tables sat welded to the floor near a fountain frothing with Cook County tap water. A window two stories tall offered awkward and unintended vantages of the adjacent skyscrapers.

The two dollar burrito that I bought to pay for my seat and the view of the city tasted like gravel in comparison to the one I had eaten the night before. As I chewed on the stale tortilla I thought of the dinner party I had attended in the Little Village, which I was told is the heart of Chicago's Mexican community. Our host was Michelle's friend Alix, herself a Chicana, who told us about how the planned amnesty for illegal immigrants to apply for US citizenship had vanished without a trace in the second week of September.

"A lot of the older women in the community don't like the fact that I'm trying to organize, to put pressure on Washington to reinstate the program," said Alix, placing dishes on the table. "A lot of people here are really fearful of the *migre*. No one wants to come forward. They'd rather remain anonymous than face deportation." On the table was homemade salsa and guacamole, fresh cut tomatoes, peppers, and lettuce. Wrapped in a fresh tortilla, it proved to be the best meal of my trip.

A janitor sweeping near my table dropped his dust pan and apologized with a coughed "Sorry." His face was dark and creased with deep smile lines. His hair was white and he couldn't have been a day under seventy. He looked at my table, which was clean of any scraps of food, as I diligently ate what fell from my burrito.

He leaned forward and spoke to me in an accent I couldn't place. "These people," he lamented, indicating the few other occupants of the food court, "they drop forty percent of their food. They eat only sixty percent. They're pigs!"

I nodded in agreement.

Outside the giant window I watched the rain clouds as they rose and fell. The rain persisted but it was warm inside. Hidden speakers spewed elevator music that was swallowed by the cavernous ceiling and the gurgle of the fountain.

As school let out for the day the rain fell upon the Young Chicago Authors, scattered in all corners of the city. Michelle ran to the shelter of the El station trying not to get soaked through. On the city's outskirts, the rainwater collected in the reservoir that feeds the pipes hidden behind every wall. Eventually this precipitation would feed the coffee maker at Rosalita's Cozy Corner. It would dilute the paint as Alex coloured the last walls of his miniature city. It would be lapped up nervously by Rocko from his bowl. Eventually the water would makes it way up to the eighth floor of this building, filling the bucket in which the aged janitor was now soaking his mop.

As he began to navigate his way across the marble floor, the janitor in his white shirt and black pants looked up at one of the fake palm trees. He paused for a second, maybe to remember his homeland. Maybe somewhere warm.

(Ghost Pine #8: Wolf, 2004)

PORT AUTHORITY

"RISE AND SHINE LADIES AND GENTLEMAN. THE TIME IS NOW FIVE o'clock in the a.m. Right now we're driving through one of New York City's fastest growing neighbourhoods. To our left you will see a new Chemical Bank. Look here, Blockbuster Video just opened a new twenty-four-hour location. And that green sign on the corner there is a brand new Starbucks.

"Ladies and gentlemen, welcome to Harlem! Yes this is Harlem, and when I lived here there weren't any banks for twenty blocks. But ever since Bill Clinton moved in things sure have been turning around, and now people like me can't afford to live here no more." In New York City Greyhound bus drivers are experts on the political and economic forces behind gentrification.

"Enough with the commentary, old man," a slowly waking passenger heckled.

"Now sir," the bus driver spoke into the PA calmly, with a velvety voice, "I didn't drive seventy miles an hour all night from Boston just to take abuse from you."

"Uh huh, that's right," a passenger spoke her appreciation.

"My man!" Her seat mate added.

The crowded bus slowly came to life as Harlem rolled past our windows. Housing projects as wide as city blocks towered out of sight. Rolled-down steel doors covered every storefront on either side of the street for miles. The sky passed from black to pre-dawn blue. In the back of the bus a den of hip-hoppers came out of hibernation, each over six feet tall and built thick. They wore matching street gear and looked like a family of bears. They began to freestyle and occasionally yelled "Y'all believe in the real hip-hop!?" as the other riders chatted in half a dozen different languages.

I thought it would be one long hall, in the tradition of the ancient train stations of America, with a thousand different platforms. Instead, Port Authority Bus Terminal was a dozen small levels, each housing fifty or so doors. These doors were portals to every town in America. The destination and schedule was posted above them, and no matter what the destination, a long line of people (mostly sleeping) and their ragtag luggage stretched behind it.

"This is America's brain," I thought, half asleep and wandering the halls in a daze. The millions of connections, from one bus to the next, of the people shooting through the nation's highways were all organized from this underground bus station. Port Authority was littered with ticket stands and newspaper stands, but mostly it was filled with the tired. The tired seem to be America's largest demographic, and yet they exert only entropy, sleep, and dreams as the expression of their political will. At this particular six a.m. this voting block seemed to be a near-unanimous majority.

Here we are; in between sleep and waking. Any number of small stresses had tired we the people out, swallowed us up and turned us into human traffic. We were migrants fleeing the war zones of our lives or trying to outrun the devil.

"Everything is orange," I thought as the escalator pulled me up to the next level. I looked for my connection to D.C., crossing beneath miles of florescent lights, trying not to get lost. Then I heard the sound of sneakers slapping across the floor behind me. Someone was running toward me.

"Jeff!" It was Molly, the only person I knew in all the five boroughs.

"Hey," I said, nonplussed. "How d'ya know I was here?"

"I didn't," she caught her breath. "I just got off the bus from Ottawa." It's almost impossible to believe, but after over twenty years as a born and raised Brooklynite, Molly was turning her back on her cultural heritage. And what paradise could have lured Molly away from this celebrated centre of American culture and power? Ottawa, Ontario; my hometown.

"It's real good to see you. Stuff like this never happens when I travel..." I tried to string together a sentence. Even when I have a movie moment, like running into the one person I know in a city of eighteen million in the bowels of Port Authority Bus Terminal, I'm still tired and frazzled.

We sat together by a newsstand for half an hour. I was

so tired I carelessly spilled a half-full bottle of apple juice, a golden puddle forming on the floor.

"I gotta catch a train to Brooklyn. I gotta pack up my house and move in two days," Molly said, standing up.

"Yeah, I gotta catch a bus to Tampa. See you back in town."

It was another hour wait before I was back on the steel dog again, speeding up a ramp and into the first natural light I had seen since the day before. The bus drove out of the fluorescent Death Star of the Port Authority, through the Lincoln Tunnel and onto the Turnpike, above the cartoonish excess of industrial New Jersey. Looking back through my window at the island I could see a giant column of smoke, thick, grey, and impenetrable, continually rising into the clouds above Manhattan.

(Two Dollars Comes With Mixtape #2, 2003)

DJANGO'S ROOM

THE LAST TIME I WAS IN SAN FRANCISCO SPIKE AND I MET MY PEN pal Erick at the sixteenth and Mission BART station where a generator show was scheduled to take place. Instead, the owner of the generator failed to appear, inspiring the listless sitting of punks on their skateboards.

Spike and I had been up packing all through the night before and were spaced. As Erick sipped from a forty ounce bottle of iced tea and we chatted with our host Melissa, to whom we'd just been introduced, a frantic woman appeared on the scene. She made a bee line for Erick, talking to him until he nodded and she continued onto the other knots of punks on the block.

Erick explained, "She's trying to enlist some folks to help move a family who just got evicted. I told her you guys just got off a plane from Canada and hadn't slept, so it's up to you."

An hour and a couple of samosas later we were knee deep in stuff in a small Mission home, trying to box it up or throw it out. We each picked a room and got to work, Erick and Melissa in the kitchen, Spike in the teenaged daughter's room, leaving me with Django, an eleven-year-old boy. All our work was overseen by Jimmy, a lifelong mover and junk collector.

Django had just finished a softball game before coming home to pack up his room with a stranger. He was a pack rat, just like I was at that age. He deliberated on every item—plastic toys, stacks of receipts from his favourite grocery store, folded up programs from the SF MoMA—before I placed it either in the garbage bag at my feet or in one of the boxes spread across the room.

There were pennies scattered on the floor, in between the sheets of his bed and even in his softball cleats, as if there had been a copper rain in his room. They were collected in a small pile. "These we keep," I explained.

At first I let him keep far too much. When his collection of plastic jack o'lanterns was on the chopping block he said "Oh I can't get rid of them, I need them for an art project."

Jimmy, overhearing as he walked down the hall, peeked into the room and said "Fuck, Django. You don't need that shit!"

"But, but..." His eyes sparkled as he scrambled to think up a valid excuse for keeping the gaudy candy receptacles.

Jimmy walked across the room, grabbed the o'lanterns and dropped them into the garbage bag. He said "Don't let him get away with too much," and handed me a beer.

Once Jimmy left the room I pulled one plastic pumpkin from the garbage and put it in a box. Django smiled and we continued dismantling his world.

For me at that age, with my elaborate systems of comic books, pamphlets and notebooks—organized in a way that seemed chaotic to anyone but myself—such a violation would have been unthinkable. And yet here was Django, forced to debate the value of each of his possessions, cheerfully letting me do just that: the unthinkable.

Of all the ephemera that I sorted that evening the only object I remember with any clarity was a bent-up poster that I unrolled. It was Frida Kahlo's self portrait with Diego Rivera.

"Oh, keep that, keep that!" Django repeated the phrase that he had said to me more than any other since I met him a few hours earlier. "That's my favourite poster," he told me, and stood next to where I sat on his bunk bed, both of us looking at the painters holding hands. One painter was gigantic, holding brushes and a palette and looking almost menacing. The other painter was birdlike and her head was slightly tilted.

Something about seeing that image of calm in the midst of the chaos of Django's room gave it a certain urgency. It wasn't a painting, but a real life tableau; the artists were standing in Django's room. I wanted to tell Frida and Diego what was going on and how I felt about it, but instead I just rolled them up and put them in a box.

The insanity of what I was doing began to sink in. Even though I knew that I was helping I still felt like an ogre tearing apart a child's room. Django's family's stay of eviction was rejected was because it couldn't be processed due to the three day holiday American civil servants took to mourn the death of Ronald Reagan. From beyond the grave he was still dispossessing the country's poor.

I retreated to the kitchen to get a jar to collect the strewn pennies. As he wrapped mugs in newspaper, Erick said to Melissa "I had this weird dream last night where we were packing all this stuff frantically and Jeff from Canada was there. Strange."

Finding a jar for the pennies and a beer in the fridge, I went back to tearing apart Django's room.

(Ghost Pine #10: Wires, 2006)

LEBANON

ALLY AT THE WHEEL AND I RIDING SHOT CRASHED INTO A CAR under an overpass outside of Lebanon, New Hampshire. We were going around thirty miles an hour and it was the other guy's fault. We were in a rental car, though, and the chemical explosion of the air bag and the bumper falling off rendered it undriveable. State trooper called the car rental franchise at the airport; closed at five. It was 5:28.

We waited an hour for our taxi to arrive and it took us to

a motel in what the husband and wife team in the front seat called "West Leb." I called my dad, who had no idea I had left my house in Montreal, and told him "Dad, I'm in Lebanon."

My father spent time in Beirut before the war and had told me "It was the Paris of the Middle East. Don't know if it's like that now, though," a couple of times.

"Lovely," he said. "How are you enjoying it?"

"It's nice," I said, before explaining.

The next day Ally and I woke early, getting to the tiny Lebanon Municipal Airport terminal as it opened up for the day. Ally talked with the clerk manning the rental desk who was a new hire and an imbecile and needed to call his manager in.

As we waited Ally collated copies of the new issue of her zine. The airport was devoid of travellers; only service industry workers gossiped over coffee on a Saturday morning.

The security detail arrived. Two US Army troops in green camo head to toe, holding shiny black machine guns. They walked around waiting, everyone just fucking waiting these last few years, talking to each other. Both gun-(they were huge black shiny things, like bad science fiction) toting soldiers were younger than me and the one I saw up close looked as if he'd never dragged a razor cross his face.

After all these years of listening to the rhetoric claiming some subversive nature of zines, North American *samizdat* and the rebellion of it all, I felt completely denuded. Here were the zines folding and there were the guns walking. Something had changed. It was 8:05 and I hadn't even had a fucking drink of coffee. What a hell of a way to wake up.

(Ghost Pine #9: Bees, 2005)

5

"DREAMED A DREAM
BY THE OLD CANAL"

THE WHEELS CLICKED OVER GROOVES IN THE BRIDGE EVERY three seconds. The van, weighed down in the back, bounced in time. As Robbie and I crossed the St. Lawrence River to the island of Montreal my watch read just past six p.m. and a late summer sun burned low in the west.

The sun is also getting low over the French vessel Saint Nicholas, creaking down the river with Ile Ste. Hélène in full view ahead. Whitecaps dot the river, it's late September and winter is already making its presence felt. On deck kneels a man, all of eighteen years old, his head hanging over the starboard rail. Two goddamn months, he's thinking, on this boat in the Atlantic! It barely held together. And he looks like he's barely held together too. He holds his stomach, but few sailors on deck give him the sympathetic looks he's fishing for. Most watch the north shore, waiting excitedly.

"Maybe five years is long enough to put that girl out of my mind," he mumbles to himself, lamenting another broken heart. A nearby sailor, involuntarily listening to the man's mumblings, hears something to the effect of "My best friend stole my girl, man I was humiliated all the way across the ocean blue. Shit."

The colony comes into view slowly, a wooden fort, a small hospital that doubles as a church and, further up the hill, a small wooden chalet encased by tall walls. "That's it?" One sailor noted his disappointment. Others on board manage more enthusiasm and soon everyone is yelling and cheering. The doors of the fort burst open, the residents jog to the point, returning the ship's call. One woman repeatedly yells "Bienvenue!" and arythmically beats a black pan with a spoon as the ship lumbers to the landing at Pointe-à-Callière.

The mumbling man stands slowly, taking in the view of the island, a blanket of green covering everything, from the foot of the river to the mountain high in the distance. The boat lurches as jagged waves beat the hull, and the man's stomach turns again. He bends, and finally pukes his guts out into the river. The year is 1653, the colony is Ville Marie, now known as Montreal, and the man, mumbling and puking, is Jean Gervais, my oldest known ancestor. Once ashore he actually lived the cliché and kissed the ground. His shipmates stared in horror.

Why am I telling you this, this vague family history? Only because my Dad wouldn't let me forget the lower branches of my family tree as I prepared to move. "If any of those bastards give you a hard time you can tell 'em all to go to hell. You're as pure laine as they come!" He was convinced I would be lynched by an unruly mob of separatists at my first utterance of English.

To my father I wasn't just moving onto greener pastures. Instead I was dispossessed Québécois returning to what Cartier called The Land of Cain, my ancestral home and my birthright.

"I watched a train set the night on fire!" my Pogues tape spat out of the van's stereo as we hit the outskirts. The roadside was littered with short buildings of concrete and chrome, holding the headquarters of pharmaceutical manufacturers and failed computer-related businesses. Large billboards rubbed against the highway, advertising Korean automobiles, Canadian doughnut shops, and more than a dozen different brands of liquor.

Closer to the city we passed the freight yard, a miniature city built of giant Lego blocks labeled CPR or CN, with indecipherable numbers across their sides. Long trains rolled slowly about the chaotic yard, taking orders from a blue and white striped control tower in the centre.

"I met my love by the gas works wall!" The autoroute rose higher on stilts until we could see the whole south-west of the island. We caught brief glimpses of people's lives through their windows, framed like a photograph.

"Dreamed a dream by the old canal," Robbie and I sang as we drove past the old canal and adjacent abandoned factories, past eighty foot tall trees and storefronts filled with only *Local à Louer* signs. We pulled up to our new apartment and sat in the van for a while. Robbie flicked off the tape and we sat in silence.

At the end of the street, fifteen feet from our front door, were two thick white concrete pillars, supporting the humming roadway seventy feet above. Our new house: the last on a dead end street, on the wrong side of the aqueduc and the wrong side of the tracks, a dozen feet from being directly beneath the autoroute. As the sunlight faded Robbie pulled his key from the ignition. Night took over.

(Ghost Pine #6, 2001)

HARVEST

ON AND OFF IT FLICKERED, THE SIGN ACROSS THE STREET. A bulldog taking a piss over and over, a column of yellow neon blinking in the night.

"I'm so sick of this eighties retro bullshit!" Madeleine fumed as the music seeped through the walls of the dog piss bar. The dog now relieved itself to the beat of "1999" by Prince. "Turn it down!" Madeleine yelled to no response.

Emily, sitting at the kitchen table, continued her story, "I'm going to get sick of it, but it'll be worth it, being up there in those big rigs with the ladies of the road. I've got two rides set up, one from Portland to L.A., then across the desert to Tucson." Her extensive fall travel plans were devoted entirely to her research into the lives of women truckers.

After moving my paltry possessions into the apartment, we had hopped across town to pick up Robbie's gear. As we car-

ried his boxes down a fire escape we were watched by a line of
six girls on an adjacent roof.

"Hey," Robbie waved to one with a freshly shaven head, before
they all disappeared inside. The van full, Robbie inserted the
key in the ignition, then pulled it out, saying, "Fuck it, there's a
party going on." We proceeded up the neighbouring fire escape.

"You guys mind sesame tofu with broccoli?" asked Madeleine, calm in the midst of cooking a meal. Madeleine was the
girl Robbie waved to, his neighbour for the last four months.
Emily and the other girls milling about were her friends, visiting from the Pacific coast. They were getting antsy.

"How long 'til dinner?"

"This recipe takes at least an hour..."

"I need to test out my new dollar store bathing cap!" All
agreed some swimming was in order.

"I gotta stay and cook this," Madeleine said as they filed out
of her room in one-piece bathing suits. We stayed, I cut broccoli and Robbie offered to do dishes. When the food was done
we were too hungry to wait for the swimmers, so we sat on a
flattened cardboard box on the roof, eating plate after plate.

When Robbie began washing dishes he said "Hot water sure
is great, huh?"

"Hm," I agreed. Madeleine nodded.

"This time last year I was back on the farm," he continued
his train of thought.

"Yeah, how was that?"

"Well at first me and Hana had been living in this nice old
camper van, it was reserved for couples, so when she left I was
demoted to sleeping in a chicken coop," he said.

At the age of seventeen Robbie talked his parents into believing it was a good idea to let him hitchhike to Winnipeg, a good
thousand miles down the road. His travelling companion
was Hana, an anarchist a full five years older than him. They
started down the road as friends, but by the time they reached
the halfway mark at the Ontario-Manitoba border they
were something more. Hana seduced Robbie and he lost his

virginity in a two man pup tent in Wawa. Or was it Kenora? The Sault? The Lakehead? All those Trans-Canada towns blur together in my mind. Whatever town it was, the forests were dark green, the rock faces light pink, and the drives between cities take days.

After two years of hanging out on and off, Hana took off to work on the Florida coast for a while. But now after a long summer apart she and Robbie were getting back to where they first fell for each other, the road.

"We're going south down the eastern seaboard, working on some organic farms on the way. We'll miss harvest though," he explained to me over tea the day before he left town. It was a sober goodbye; summer was over.

"I'll be back by spring and we can tour, don't sweat it."

We spent most of the spring and summer together while Hana was away. I was the loyal roadie to "Robbie Rockshow," his one man band. He played all manner of folk and punk tunes, songs that managed to be both urgent and timeless. His guitar had a red circle-A sticker and a flimsy pick-up, stuck on with bubble gum. Out in the crowd I sang along to his cover of the John Denver song "Take Me Home, Country Roads."

Singing along was but one of my duties. I also lugged around the heavy roadcase and secured our means of transportation by sticking out my thumb. The plan was to avoid cities and 400-series highways, sticking to the back roads. We were blazing a trail across the Ottawa Valley and the St. Lawrence Seaway, making friends with farmers and townies. We were eventually going to stay out for whole seasons, doing research in the libraries by day and playing on a different porch every night.

In the end we only managed to reach the cafés, youth centres, and basements of half a dozen towns.

Robbie and Hana's trip suffered the same fate as our tour. They made it as far as an anarchist farm outside of Portland, Maine, before she got cold feet and they parted ways, this time for good. Hana followed through with their plan, which was really her plan, and went to Mexico. Robbie stayed in Maine until the harvest was in.

In Madeleine's kitchen Robbie is smiling or maybe wincing. "Yeah it was originally a chicken coop. It'd been renovated so the wind couldn't get it, but it did, and it was October, pretty draughty. Me and Hana'd planned to be in Mexico by then so I only had a summer sleeping bag. Every morning I woke up and the walls were dripping condensation and I could see my breath."

Robbie grabbed a wok from the sink and began to scrub. "I remember one week at the tail end of harvest I got stuck with dishwashing duty in the kitchen. There was no hot water and to conserve energy the farm's power went out at six p.m. There were stacks and stacks of dishes, so I always ended up busting suds with cold water, in the dark."

He turned on an element on the stove to dry the wok.

"Sounds rough," said Madeleine.

"Yeah… rough," Robbie said, as if realizing it for the first time.

"Hey Robbie," I pipe up. "D'ya ever think about shackin' up with Hana for a while before you took off on your trip? Not living in the same house, but at least the same city. I mean she'd been away a pretty long time, and the road ain't always the best place to get reacquainted."

"Hm," Robbie looked at me thoughtfully. He turned off the stove, picked up the wok, and stacked it on top of the rack of drying dishes. "I need some cigarettes," he said as he walked onto the fire escape. Madeleine and I watched the precariously-placed wok wobble and shiver, hitting the kitchen floor just as Robbie hit the street.

The problem with falling in love with a traveller is easy to figure out. They keep moving, even after they've sworn you their heart. You become another town with a funny name they can say they've been to or a city they're anxious to leave, a stifling neighbourhood a few thousand miles back, disappearing fast from their rearview mirror.

Across the street the dog piss flickered on and off.

(Ghost Pine #6, 2001)

FASCISTS

I EYED THE STACK OF DUSTY LPS IN THE BACK OF THE CROWDED room. "Ça coute combien?" I asked as I began to flip through them.

"One dollar each," the grey haired man at the cash replied. "But I don't have to sell them to you."

Montreal. The rent is so cheap that middle aged men rent storefronts to sell off their life after their wives finally leave them. Rather than sort things out they put everything on the floor and decide what to keep only when a customer wants to buy. They sell off the remains of their own personal apocalypse, and take a liking to it.

This trouvaille was one of half a dozen junk shops on rue de L'Église, near my house. Translated the street name means 'of the church,' but its namesake looked more like a cathedral. Its hulking frame anchored the east end of the street, another relic of the province's crumbling devotion to Catholicism. It's been over thirty years since the Québécois began abandoning their church like a sinking ship. A few neighbourhood women regularly fill the pews, but only those with white hair remember the rush that comes with fearing God.

Rue de L'Église fared little better than its eponym, though it remained the main artery of Verdun, a neighbourhood with a rich history which decayed appropriately. All fall I had to dodge speeding cars since the crosswalk signs were broken. An old man posted his open letter on telephone poles, lamenting days gone by when both French and English took pride in the neighbourhood. He derided the mayor's "surrender of once thriving Verdun to the woes of careless fiscal planning." As if to assuage the poor crank, further down the road a decade-old sign in front of a burnt-out rowhouse optimistically predicted "Coming Soon: Condominiums!"

Walking up de L'Église the first time I found a closed-up movie theatre, a closed bowling alley, an 'authentic British fish 'n chips shop' where the waitress didn't speak English, and a post office where the two moustache-wearing men bickered like an old married couple. One man's moustache was white, the other's black.

I also found six barbershops, where haircutters in white shirts sat in their chairs reading *Le Journal*, waiting.

The empty buildings were covered in graffiti. Unlike the author of the open letter the last generation had grown up knowing their neighbourhood in decline. I studied the faded tags in blue and green krylon.

One day I noticed a storefront window painted with the words H. Letourneau Velos. I went home and got Grace then walked inside, breathing in the grease and noticing the line of ten speeds across the back wall. The room sat completely silent, apart from the soft ring of a bell as the door closed behind me.

"Bonjour," said H. Letourneau as he emerged from the back room. "Qu'est-ce qui se passe?" he asked me softly.

Two generations ago he would have been a lumberjack or a blacksmith. The sleeves of his shirt were rolled up, revealing arms as thick as Christmas hams. Suspenders held up his thick wool pants and a pair of black spectacles curled around his ears. Atop his six-foot-five frame sat a wreath of white hair.

"J'avais un accident," I said, pointing to my scarred chin. He looked at the beat up ten speed I dragged through the door, sizing it up. Handle bar bent on the right side, a brake cable pulled from its socket, the front wheel about to fall off, and most notably, brown bloodstains on the length of the frame.

He picked up the bicycle and righted the handlebar with sheer brute force. Pulling out his toolbox to fix the other ailments, he worked swiftly and efficiently, as if playing an instrument.

"Where are you from?" he asked in a lightly accented voice.

"Ottawa, I just moved here last week."

"Mon frère habite à Orleans. I love to go see the colours of leaves in the fall at Gatineau Park."

"I do too, but the last time I tried to go see the leaves I didn't get there until midnight," I said.

He smiled and told me the price of the repairs as he put away his tools.

"Vignt-six?" I asked, fully ready to pay him twenty-six dollars.

"No, you misunderstand. Two dollars and sixty cents."

I paid him with a handful of change. He put the money in his pocket, not in the green cash register perched on the counter. I thanked him and headed for the door, but he stopped me to read what was scrawled across the frame of my bike. It was covered in blood, but the sharpie'd words were still legible.

"This machine kills fascists," he read aloud. Then he pointed to the scar on my chin, visible through a few days of stubble.

"It looks like the fascists almost killed you!" he laughed.

(Ghost Pine #6, 2001)

DRAG IT TO DINNER

"ON A CLEAR DAY I SWEAR YOU CAN SEE ALL THE WAY TO NEW Brunswick," he said from the kitchen as I shivered outside, on his thirty-first-floor balcony.

I stared out, past cobblestoned Old Montreal, to the concrete grain silos in the distance, the red neon Farine Five Roses sign flickering. I stepped inside the apartment and closed the sliding door behind me, a steaming plate of gluten buffalo wings waiting at my place setting.

"Back on the farm in Indiana my mom taught me how to make gluten. We'd put wheat to soak in big barrels, all winter. My poor mother, such a terrible cook," he laughed. Edmund Syam: radio host, antique car enthusiast, amateur painter, fourth generation vegetarian, cookbook writer, and now my boss. This was our second weekly meeting to construct a publishing calendar and taste-test the new recipes. I was finally getting paid to work in the dicey world of independent publishing, ten bucks an hour under the table.

It was a grey November morning, and I slept right through it, my alarm going off at noon sharp. "Aw, shit," was my first thought of the day. I promised Robbie I would be at his workshop, and I was already late. I grabbed the last day's t-shirt and jeans and ran to the metro station.

Robbie worked at the Frigo Vert, a health food store funded by the university. In their mission to fulfill the students' needs they maintained a well hidden location and prohibitively high prices, and stocked only the most obscure ancient grains in their bulk bin. Today, in one of Robbie's attempts at reaching out to the student body, the store was hosting a vegan dessert-cooking seminar featuring some local celebrity. It was starting at noon sharp.

The rain poured and turned the steep streets into huge concrete waterslides. I was soaked as I walked into the Frigo Vert's test kitchen located behind a shelf stacked with twelve different brands of miso. I looked around the room, hoping to see some familiar faces from the city's thriving free food scene.

"Hello! Who are you?" A two hundred and fifty pound bald middle-aged man with a Midwestern accent addressed me. He stood in the middle of the kitchen next to Robbie.

"Uh... I'm Jeff."

"I'm Edmund." There were only three other people in the tiny kitchen and he introduced me to all of them before continuing to give directions on how to make chocolate tofu cheesecake.

"Now we add some soy milk. The soy milk says... moo!" He mooed as he poured half a carton into a metal mixing bowl.

After the demonstration I munched on all of the three desserts prepared in hopes of a larger audience. Edmund cleared his throat and spoke up. "If anyone would like to buy copies of my two cookbooks, just ask. Also I'll be looking for an assistant in the near future." I made a mental note of this job offer, followed by a quick exit. The cheesecake had dwindled and Robbie was on the prowl. "Hey, anyone wanna do dishes?"

"Here are some pictures of me at Unity." He handed me an album of pictures featuring a buxom woman with flowing locks in a black party dress. "My drag name is Yolande. I'm so trash." I chewed on the latest chocolate chip cookie recipe for the new all-dessert cookbook. "I wrote a proposal for a TV production company. I want to do a cooking show as Yolande, the Tofu Temptress. I had the best name for it too: Drag it to Dinner! They never got back to me."

Only a month had passed since our first meeting and I already had business cards, my position as Vice President of Sales appearing beneath my name. I called stores to expand distribution, with occasional compromises. The queer bookstore on the Main wouldn't take any copies until we made stickers for the cover which read "Gay Food is Good Food" over a pink triangle.

At the next meeting we ate sweet and sour tofu, a recipe from Edmund's friend in Brazil. "Did you say you were from Ottawa?" Edmund asked. I nodded. "That's where I had my honeymoon!" I blinked. "Fresh out of teachers' college I took a job offer to be a principal at an elementary school in Newfoundland. They had no teachers back then, poor Newfies. It was a Catholic school, so the unwritten rule was to fill the position I'd need a lovely wife by my side. Of course I knew I wasn't exactly in the vagina business, but I married a girl from school anyway. She was absolutely crazy about me. When I popped the question she nearly fainted. I think she knew about me even then. We had a small service.

"There were these cabins you could rent near Parliament Hill. The first night I had terrible butterflies in my stomach. She took her clothes off and it was the first time I'd ever seen a pussy. I threw up! Can you believe it? Poor Doreen, I cried all night and eventually spat out the truth. She was the first person I ever came out to. My wife.

"The next day we moved to Newfoundland, where I was the school principal for five years and Doreen had some wonderful affairs with the local men." He paused, "How old are you, Jeff?"

"Twenty."

"All that happened when I was nineteen. Just nineteen." He looked out the window.

The January thaw came quick, submerging the streets in slush five feet deep. Edmund and I were attempting to ford a particularly deep puddle as we tried to make our way to the university across town. The prestigious university, not the liberal university that funded health food stores and bicycle libraries. Edmund had been asked to give a talk on veganism to the environmental club, and it seemed as good an opportunity to schlep cookbooks as any.

I wore a dirty skidoo jacket and Edmund was covered by a black trench coat and a fedora and we scaled ten foot snowbanks together in a hurry. Edmund pointed to a cathedral on the corner. "I lived there when I was working on my Master's and my friend Aaron lived there too. We both did custodial work for room and board. The head caretaker loved the idea of a fag and a Jew living in a church together."

Black clouds began to circle and night fell prematurely, the puddles crusting over with a thin film of ice. Silence fell, so I tried to make conversation. "Edmund, how did you start writing cookbooks? I guess you just wanted to get the word out about veganism?"

"Cookbooks? Well... they say that a fag's hometown is wherever they first come out. So this is my hometown. When I first moved here I couldn't believe how many people were just like me. How many men! Those first years here were just like heaven. I lived in the Village and never left. The life just consumed me. I barely completed my doctorate. I had a lot of good friends."

"But the eighties were different," he continued, "One by one I lost them. My hair turned grey. There was no one left."

"Five years ago I wanted to do something. I wanted to remember the way we lived, wine and dancing, and I remembered all the meals I cooked. So I wrote up the recipes my friends loved, twenty-four recipes for twenty-four friends gone. I printed only enough copies to give to their partners or their mothers, if they were on good terms."

"I wanted to remember the way we lived," he repeated.

We arrived at the campus and after a half hour of frantic searching we found the room. I set up a merchandise table, just like any night on tour with a band, looking to sell people a souvenir.

He looked around the still empty room. "I wonder if there will be any cute boys in attendance tonight." He grinned. "Present company excluded, of course."

I blushed.

(Ghost Pine #6, 2001)

MOVIES AND BIKES

THERE WAS A WAR BEING WAGED THAT WINTER, UP AND DOWN Ste. Catherine, pitched campaigns from cinema to cinema. The last bastions of cheap flicks, movie houses that had stood for decades were now falling at an alarming rate.

The culprit was the new multiplex, the Paramount at the corner of Metcalfe Street. After only a year of operation it was well on its way to becoming the busiest theatre in North America. Housed behind the façade of an old office building sat ten screens, equipped with digital everything, and seats that rivaled the posh patent leather chairs at the Westmount Public Library for comfort.

The first victim was the Loews cinema, the best place to catch Sunday matinees of arty Hollywood movies. The Loews was a great place to take your girl on a date—an empty theatre was guaranteed, allowing dubious acts of love to go unnoticed. It tanked during the dry spell between Christmas and early spring Oscar-mania.

Next to collapse was the Cinema Centre-Ville, a vintage dive left over from the seventies. The screen was as big as a high school classroom's chalkboard, and it hung before thirty broken-down seats. Acoustic panels the colour of nicotine stains hung from the walls.

A two-dollar matinee found me and Heather watching the sad tale of an old man driving to his long lost brother's house.

Nearly all of the theatre's seats were filled with the typical weekday matinee audience, the idle rich and the unemployed. Usually the two groups mix like oil and water, but hell, everyone loves movies!

The Centre-Ville was difficult to locate, and therein lay most of its charm. It was located inside a subway station, completely separate from the snowy streets above. It was a cinema speakeasy. Unfortunately its well-hidden, subterranean location did little to protect it from the bloodbath topside.

The last bastion of cheap movies downtown was the Palace, holding three massive screens. Both management and patrons did everything possible to contradict its regal name. I heard tales of sex in the bathrooms, sex in the aisles, spitting on the floor, crazies yelling at the screen, couples breaking up and cursing at each other, fist fights, knife fights and gang warfare breaking out in the middle of movies.

None of the stories I heard were first hand, but something about the place made you believe every urban legend. Maybe it was the hip-hop blasting from the concession stand, or the dozens of people in tear-away track suits and skull-caps standing by the bathroom doors. Whatever it was, something was definitely happening.

At the Palace all you needed was two measly bucks to watch ninety minutes of second-run Hollywood bullshit. You'd hate it if you had paid a cent more, but you'd remind yourself you get what you pay for and that somehow makes it okay. Most people got in line before they read the marquee.

I went on Palace deathwatch as soon as management dared to change the classic two dollar ticket, jacking it up to a whopping three bucks. Then a few days after I warmed myself up by watching a movie about the desert, the last film can was filled and the Palace turned off its sign for good.

Thursday nights I did a three-hour shift volunteering at the bike tool library. The night of my first shift I couldn't find the place, so I found Robbie instead.

"What do you mean you can't find it, it's so obvious," he said, leading me to the end of a dark alley, pointing to a doorway beneath an icy staircase and a bare light bulb.

Inside Grant asked me "Are you a mechanic?"

"Uh... no."

"Are you mechanically minded? At all?"

Following a long silence he pointed to a stack of mouldy magazines in a dark corner of the concrete room. "We're planning to turn that into a library, someone just donated all those bike mags. Wanna organize 'em?"

That was me, the librarian of the bikeshop. A square peg in a round hole. But every Thursday night, through rain, sleet, or hail, I was there, bringing order to the last twenty years of *Cycle* and *Bicycling* magazines. I even managed to slip in a copy of my own zine, once it was printed.

The shop was run on funds provided by the university, but most students had no idea it existed. If the students did find it, the bikes they wanted fixed looked more like they needed to be put down. Instead, it was overrun by bike messengers in bright rain jackets, cut-off shorts, and wrap-around sunglasses.

The messenger mechanics told stories of life on the road as they worked. This wasn't the same almighty 'road' constantly glorified by dilettante travellers. This road was the city, all of its streets populated by hard-working alcoholics, eccentrics, gearheads, fuck ups, intellectuals and ordinary folk. All manner of people found a bit of acceptance in the hydraheaded messenger underground, and they all talked about the road the way fisherman talk about the sea.

"Shit, another winter. This is going to be my eleventh on the road, and my last. I swear to fuckin' God."

"Do you guys remember Li'l Billy?" Someone nodded. "Well, his bike got stolen so he'd been riding a loaner 'til payday. So payday comes and rather than heading straight to the bike shop he gets the bright idea that he needs a few drinks. He wakes up the next morning in an alleyway, his bike's gone, so's the cash he had for the new one, and he has no idea what happened.

"And you wanna know the worst part? The loaner he was riding was my winter bike! I mean Christ! You can't trust no one." He laughed bitterly.

I may have been there every Thursday, but I didn't fit in, nor did I want to. I never dared bring Grace in to work on for fear of being laughed out of the room. Instead I kept the library in order, colour-coded the tools, and watched from the sidelines as volunteer mechanics performed miracles on collapsing bicycles.

At eleven o'clock I coasted down the mountain and then along the Lachine Canal. Its surface was placid and grey; at its bottom sat a foot and a half of thick toxic sediment. A layer of cadavers and chemicals, left over from when abattoirs and paint factories lined the banks. The canal was sealed off from the river, but in three years' time it would open again, the sediment sealed beneath a tarp, to pleasure boats rather than barges.

The once-deserted factories were now covered in scaffolding. Graffiti on a nearby wall read "Gentrification: Coming soon to a ghetto near you."

(Ghost Pine #6, 2001)

POINTE ST. CHARLES

I DON'T KNOW IF IT RAINS MORE IN THE POINTE THAN ANYWHERE else on the island, but it sure feels that way. It's not uncommon to return home from sunny downtown to find a downpour in the south.

This is a good place to wear a raggedy sweater and bushwhack through the underbrush with the dog. A good time can be had by making a potato gun and trying to smash out some of the high-rise apartment windows on Ile des Soeurs a mile across the river. A good time even if the trigger on the P-gun gets jammed and won't shoot.

There's a feeling in the south-west of being somehow below the city. All the unruly hills of downtown flatten and the roads stretch to the river broken and empty.

Down here in the Pointe we make our own fun. Last time

Chaos House (pronounced CH-owse H-owse) had a party I crowd-surfed the living room to the sweet wankery of "Whole Lotta Love" while party people made out and Nic chipped Mike's tooth.

When we don't want to make our own fun we hit the cult video store across the Verdun line, renting fucked-up films from the parka-clad owners (the heat always off in an attempt to save money). We paint our living room walls blue with TV beams and the mice make daring raids on snack-foods dropped on the floor.

Karen, the waitress at the all-day breakfast place across the street from the park, knows our names and orders by heart, even the names of our houseguests.

When I walk down the industrial access road drunk off two dollar pints from the SAQ and everything is broken and dead and lying on the side of the road I couldn't be happier.

(Ghost Pine #9: Bees, 2005)

THE SECRET SAINTS OF MONTREAL

MY NEW CITY ONLY MAKES SENSE ON A BICYCLE. ON THE WAY home late at night it's all downhill. It's my one reward after spending my day climbing the city. The potholed streets drag me along through the night as I stitch the city together in my mind.

The streets pull me past the twenty-four hour bagel shops of Mile End where the sesame seed bagels fresh from the ovens melt in your hands. Tugging me past countless rowhouses and their snaking cast iron stairs. Above, laundry lines intersect the telephone poles in complex diagonals.

I speed up as the street gets steeper, down St. Urbain past Mordecai Richler's old high school, I think. And two blocks east the Main sits creaky, neon-lit and put to bed for the night.

I descend into the back alley sin of Ste. Catherine, past the barren loading docks of strip clubs and sex shops, passing the same ladies on the same block every night. I pause to put my hand in the mouth of an angry stone Chinese dragon for good luck. I pass through the gates of Chinatown, the air fills with the scent of rotting produce and the streets are lined with restaurants that never empty.

I bike faster, pretending the city is silently collapsing in my wake. The buildings and monuments are falling like dominoes and I can't look back.

I fly past the Notre-Dame Cathedral where Layton wrote his poem, and into the skinny streets of Old Montreal where by night the ghosts come out to play. I escape down the Lachine Canal bike path bordered by skeletons of industry. Across the canal sits a giant collection of grain elevators and silos topped with a red neon sign flashing the words "Farine Five Roses" into the night. I'm off the mountain now.

One midnight Robbie and I were on the final stretch of the bike path when we heard that music again, coming from an old warehouse across the canal. Every time I bike by I hear different snatches of a melodica or break beat, distorted by the wind or water.

We pulled off the path to catch the music but it was drowned out by the ring of the railway crossing. In comes the freight train on the bridge just a few yards in front of us, the boxcars reflected in the steely canal.

Nearby the Atwater Market clock tower stands tall. Under its gaze and the night's cover we steal apples and tiny pumpkins from the market's unguarded stalls. Everything tastes sweeter when it's stolen.

Behind the clock tower the city is strung with light bulbs. All the skyscrapers try to compete with the unsurpassable height of the mountain. One building is topped with a searchlight that follows the night train's path, left to right over and over the light carves its way across the sky.

And you can smell the season turn. The sky is now so fragile and thin I could tear it right down the middle. Above the glass towers stands the old cross on the older mountain. It's a million watt relic preaching to the secular city, standing sullen next to a red lit trident, a giant radio broadcast tower. Robbie says it's a memorial to Poseidon, the Greek god of the seas. Erected to remind us that this city was all under water once, under the Precambrian Champlain Sea. And it could be submerged once more, Poseidon willing.

"All the streets in this city are named after saints and murderers," Robbie says, "And some are both." Robbie's writing a book called *The Secret Saints of Montreal* about the saints streets are named after. Until he has time to research it all we go around making up our own stories about the saints, beatifying the strangers who have passed through our lives. St. Remi was a man who picked up Robbie as he hitchhiked through New Brunswick, St. Patrick was a kid I rode the bus with in grade one, I was in a punk band once with old St. Mathieu, truly sacred and amazing on a drum kit.

The real secret is that it doesn't matter about the lives of saints. The real stories have been too veiled in secrecy and worship to decipher now. And once something has been named and its story told it takes on its own reality. So St. Remi will always be a guy who picked up Robbie, the brown stone school on St. Urbain will always be the one Mordecai Richler went to. And, radio tower or not, there stands Poseidon's trident, keeping the cross company atop the mountain. Above them sits the dusty old moon nearly full, whispering the tides.

I grab one of my stolen McIntoshes and bite into it. And it's sweet and sour just like always. But this apple tastes different somehow. It has an old familiarity but still tastes fresh and new just like this city, four hundred years old but new to me.

I never knew I could be so inspired yet so confused, so alone yet so happy, so unsure of the future yet so filled with hope all at once, but this city is proving it to me. This is my life and for once it tastes right, stolen at night when no one was looking, sweet and sour and autumnal. And now I'm extending it to you. Take a bite.

(Otaku #5, 1999)

"COCKSUCKER"

MATT, WHO DESCRIBES HIS CONVERSATIONAL STYLE AS EQUAL parts abstraction and bombast, is holding court outside Open da Night after Barcelona's defeat of Arsenal.

"This motherfucking fucker almost killed me the other day," he begins calmly, gesturing in the direction of his bicycle. "He came this close to hitting me," he adds, holding his thumb and forefinger an inch apart.

"His window was open so I yell 'Cocksucker!' at him. I usually yell 'cocksucking motherfucking rat' but the guy was driving away so I had to abridge.

"So I fuckin' bike up to the next light. And I'm sitting there right next to him when he sticks his head out and calls me a homophobe."

He pauses. "And the thing is, he's absolutely right. I concede that in this situation he has the moral high ground. He almost killed me but *I'm* the asshole."

"Jezus," I say. "It must've been awkward sitting there, waiting for the light to change."

"Oh, it was," he nods.

"It was the goalie, the Spanish goalie," Myles adds in a daze. "If he didn't get a red card Arsenal would've had the game. That guy is a fucking wall."

(Ghost Pine #11: Crows, 2007)

6

UNTITLED DIALOGUE BETWEEN ME AND ME AT AGES 16 AND 24

I WAS HOME FOR CHRISTMAS, TRACING THE PATHS OF MY STUPID younger years late at night. Walking the streets I travelled as a teen brought back old thoughts and they rolled around in my mind like candy in an empty dish. The claustrophobia of the suburbs flooded in with each step. I promised myself, as I had done every night when I had acne, that soon I would leave this place forever.

Soft relief spread over me when I realized that I had transplanted my life from here years ago. The suburbs are a time-fuck. Never changing. "I'm just home for Christmas," I thought, and then began to enjoy the night for what it was. An empty calendar square at the end of a busy year.

The weather was fucked up. It was mere days until Xmas but it was raining instead of snowing and the atmosphere felt strange. So I wasn't surprised when I saw the nihilist Champion hoodie'd waif emerge from a bank of mist. He seemed very familiar.

He approached me with caution, having never encountered anyone else walking these streets after six p.m. When he took off his headphones I introduced myself. "Hi," I said. "I'm you, or *was* you." He stared at me.

For reasons I can't explain, I suddenly felt it was my duty

to infuse some hope into the youngster. "Listen," I began in a sage tone, "just hang in there."

"Are you really suggesting I listen to that clichéd piece of advice?" The teen was immediately spitting mad. "Fuck you, man. 'Hang in there'? That's what the poster in the guidance office says. The one with the cat hanging from the rope. You asshole."

"Jesus, do you have to be such a punk?" I asked the little shit. Then I remembered how much fun I'd had getting under everyone's skin, back-talking math teachers, the vice-principal and my parents alike. Being a righteous prick was my hobby at that age and I was convinced that everyone in my vicinity deserved an equal dose of my snotty vitriol. The kid, with his shaved head and acne on the chin, was ruining my misty night Hollywood time-travel moment.

Next he hit below the belt. "I can tell you're not punk any-more." My long hair and plaid shirt garnered me the derision of the teen. He was disgusted to the point of doubting that I was indeed his future self, and yet somehow he knew it was true.

"I bet you even lost edge!" he said, with something like a sob wound around his voice.

"You bet," I said, enjoying the look of disgust on his face. "Broke edge as soon as I turned nineteen and was legal to drink. My advice is don't get any 'True 'til Death' tattoos."

"God," he whispered. "At least tell me you don't smoke weed?"

I shook my head and made the 'sucking from an invis-ible roach' motion; touching my right thumb and forefinger, bringing them to my mouth and sucking in air.

"Argh! You're just like those asshole skaters who smoke up in the park. Fuck!" He continued the assault, "And what's with the hair? Are you into *grunge*, asshole?"

"Listen, you little prick. I just need you to answer one ques-tion: what the fuck are you so mad about anyway? You never worked a day in your life, you get an *allowance* for Christ's sake! C'mon, refresh my memory."

He began to explain himself. He said "It's just..." but then shook his head and stopped speaking. He clamped the plastic headphones onto his ears and pulled a black hood over his head. Before disappearing back into the mist, he extended his middle finger and waved it in my direction.

(Ghost Pine #10: Wires, 2006)

THE SOCIAL JUSTICE CLUB
Part One

[BREAKFAST]

THE KITCHEN TABLE WAS TOO SMALL TO SIT ALL FOUR MEMBERS of my family at once so we worked through breakfast in shifts, as in the galley of a crowded cargo ship. As I sipped the last of my orange juice, my father was already walking across the snow-bound park to the bus shelter. My mother, unable to sleep past five a.m., was at work in the basement laundry room and had been for hours. Upstairs my brother, the university student, was still asleep and would wake only an hour before his late afternoon class, the lucky bastard.

Drowned in milk and glittering with crystals of brown sugar, my bowl of porridge sat half-eaten on the newspaper splayed across the table. My blurry eyes scanned the black marks on the long pages. The paper was a fixture at the breakfast table; as I flipped through it full colour images of destruction caught my eye and I sleepily puzzled at the logic behind ingesting news and food at the same time.

My family kept abreast of the daily disasters not only by reading the paper at breakfast, but also by watching the six o'clock news every night. We ate our dinner on TV trays with faux wood-grain tops so we could see the story of how the world survived another day. It was narrated by men and women with perfect teeth and corporate backers. Served up over meat and potatoes the news was a kind of black gravy covering everything on our plates. No wonder half the advertisements were for heartburn medication.

My father preferred the wobbly trays to a proper table.

When he was a kid his family sat at a crowded table at dinner and whenever he said anything wrong his father boxed his ears. On those rare occasions when my family ate at the large dining room table, we sat far enough apart that no one was within arm's reach and my father often leaned back in his chair.

I tried to look for stories in the paper but all I saw were shapes and pictures, the pages broken up into rectangular blocks or long columns. None of the items connected to those they shared the page with and I could never figure my way through their labyrinthine twists and turns. My eyes were fuzzy since I hadn't wiped the sleep from them.

After reading the entire comics page without laughing once, I gave up and tossed the paper across the table. I didn't believe anything the corporate stooges at the Ottawa *Citizen* published anyway, not even *Peanuts*. I had recently seen the documentary about Noam Chomsky and knew that the media doesn't actually report what happened but instead served its corporate owners by manufacturing consent. That I knew. That and everything else in the world.

[DIARRHEA AND POMPOM]
What porridge I managed to eat sat heavy in my stomach. It was February and I was sick of the winter breakfasts that my mom prepared. Since the end of Christmas holidays breakfast had been nothing but porridge and the occasional bowl of cream of wheat.

My mother emerged from the basement stairwell, dressed in a thick floor length nightgown, decorated by a dainty bow tied over the heart.

"Mom, what is this, *Oliver Twist*?" I asked crappily, referring to the bowl of gruel in front of me.

"It's good for you," was her cheerful reply to my familiar youthful insubordination. She ascended the stairs to the second floor to retrieve the laundry hamper and passed through the kitchen again as she returned to the basement. "Sticks to your ribs!" she said, driving home her pro-porridge message.

Gruel *was* easy on my intestinal tract, an organ that had proved itself quite unreliable in the past. My body metabolized porridge effortlessly, the thick wheat grains or whatever the hell it was descending slowly into my stomach, unlike the raisin bran I ate the rest of the year. That breakfast cereal occasionally caused me violent bouts of diarrhea on the walk to school.

It would hit me halfway up the street. At first I would ignore my gurgling stomach and the waves of nausea, but within seconds I would be clenching my butt cheeks and running home. By the time I arrived the length of my stride was reduced by the squishy feeling in my pants.

"Oh Jeffy. You shit your pants!" my mom would say sympathetically. "Well, I had the runs plenty of times. Ugh." She scrunched her face. "You just feel so awful when it happens, eh?"

After setting my pants and underwear to soak she would drive me to school and compose me a note, inventing a phantom doctor's appointment so I might be admitted to class without a late marked next to my name.

I scraped the remains of my breakfast into the garbage before climbing the stairs to the bathroom. As I brushed my teeth I looked at myself in the mirror, cataloguing my flaws. My shaggy hair stood up straight in several places and a few new zits had appeared on my chin. In the winter months, when sweat was staved off by frigid weather, I rarely changed my clothes and showered only once a week, if that.

Stomping downstairs to the vestibule, I pulled my oversized parka from its hanger. Once it sat on my shoulders I activated its safeguards, snapping the inner belt and buttoning the flap across the front, to protect myself from the wind blowing up my coat or sneaking through its clenched zipper teeth.

I pulled on my backpack and stepped into knee-high black winter boots. After tying a scarf around my neck I reached into one of the boxes high on the closet shelf and grabbed my final protection from the bitter cold.

The bottom half of my toque was much like any other, white crossed by multi-coloured stripes. But what sat atop it was a piece of unrivalled artistry. While most pompoms are discreet, no larger than a few centimetres in diameter, this magical toque was crowned by a giant radiating puffball larger than the winter hat below.

Pulling it over my ears I remembered how I laughed at its sheer absurdity when I first came upon it. Before the week was out I had a change of heart and began wearing it on the walk to school. It was another month before I had guts enough to wear it inside the school corridors. The mighty pom of red, blue, yellow and orange I wore each day was a beacon of colour in the bleached winter landscape.

The hat, like all the clothes I found in my parents' boxes of seasonal accessories or in the basement, was strange and from another time. At first I wore their old jackets and shirts as a joke, but after incorporating them into my wardrobe I developed a genuine fondness for them. Kids at school called me a freak for wearing my mom's baby blue wool sweater or one of my dad's large polyester shirts. But what they didn't grasp, what they couldn't possibly understand with their puny brains was that I wasn't trying to shock anyone with my wardrobe. I genuinely liked the clothes I found in the basement.

When fully assembled, my winter ensemble resembled a space suit, albeit one with a wolf-fur fringe around the hood. My only exposed skin was seen through the eye slit between the top of my scarf tied tight against my cheekbones and the bottom of my toque just above my eyebrows.

I inserted my walkman into the breast pocket of my parka and clamped the large black headphones over my head, taking care not to intrude on the pompom's airspace. Layers of cotton, flannel and down protected me from wind and cold, but it was these headphones that wove the magical force-field around me, one that allowed me to strike out valiantly, despite doubts and an insufficient amount of sleep, into the valley of darkness that was my morning walk to school.

[PUNK ROCK AND SNOW]

Opening the front door, my lungs filled with a breath of sharp cold air. Pressing my walkman's Play button I quickly pulled on my mitts. After a moment of silence I was enveloped in a scream of guitar feedback. The tape holding the soundtrack to my trek across the barrens slowly began to unwind.

The world of homes and streets had disappeared under a desert of white. The half metre of snow erased the borders between lawn and grey asphalt. Overnight the wind had carved the powder into dunes with sensuous curves but now it rose from a brief slumber to undo its night's work, fiercely whipping the snow into the sky.

The houses lining my neighbourhood's streets were built from three different floor plans. For the most part they were distributed evenly in sets of three, but occasionally two of the same sat next to each other. The only difference between such twins was the colour of the ornamental shutters hanging on either side of their second floor windows.

As a kid growing up in my suburban neighbourhood, I liked it okay enough. But that like had long since soured into the blackest hatred. Blame punk rock. When I started going downtown to buy records at Birdman Sound or to hardcore shows at 5 Arlington I was amazed by the diversity of architecture and people. Each block was thick with apartments and storefronts, so different from the binary of homes and lawns on my suburban street.

I didn't just come to hate the suburb I grew up in, but *all* of them. They became to me the symbol of everything wrong in the world. My whinge went beyond the uniformity of the houses or lack of sidewalks; I had a problem with *everything* about them.

People didn't share. Everyone had their own lawnmower, sitting unused in the garage six days out of seven. Most of those were gas lawnmowers run by engines that coughed grey clouds of exhaust and whined like a giant wasp. Houses and stores were segregated and so to survive a car was needed to get to a grocery store kilometres away. Once you were there the produce you bought had travelled by truck even further, probably from B.C. at the closest. Suburbs are sprawling holy cities devoted to one god, oil. They are environments built with the express purpose of making life impossible for those who travel by foot.

I could go on forever, and often did, ranting about how the place my parents had chosen to raise me was stifling, oppressive and just generally sucked. There were even books on the subject that agreed with me. I hadn't read any of them, but it still meant something to know I wasn't alone in my disdain.

The dull sky opened into a flurry and the air grew dense with snow. Clinging to my lashes, large flakes refracted a rainbow of kaleidoscopic colour in my eyes as they melted. The horizon disappeared and the white on the ground merged with that in the sky. The path behind me was erased and what lay ahead was reduced to a point of hope.

"Man," I thought, "this is nowhere."

[INDIAN ROAD]
My boots found traction only in the parallel strips that had been dug into the snow by car wheels. It wasn't long before a horn penetrated my headphones and I grudgingly stepped out of the furrow, climbing up a tall snowbank.

In the blizzard the guitar, bass and drums in my ears seemed closer, they surrounded me. The snow would have sung me its own music if I had cared to listen. But the squeak of snow under my boot was cancelled out."

"This song, that song, love song, hate song / You're so bored," sang Justin Trosper. "Anything, everything, everywhere, nowhere / You're bored."

In my bedroom I had a collection of LPs that, when placed in a row, spines out, was only a few centimetres thick. Each of the black disks were engraved with my favourite kind of music: hardcore punk rock. After Christmas and my last birthday I had taken my accumulated gift money to the bank and purchased American money orders. Six to eight weeks after sending my order away to a small record label, a cardboard box would appear in the mail. These boxes bore the postmarks of such alien locales as Brattleboro, VT, Goleta, CA and Arlington, VA.

I pulled out my father's road atlas and used the index to locate the towns named on those postmarks. I stared at the place names on the maps intently, as though if I looked hard enough I could somehow understand what they were like. Rather than guess from what dark psychological recesses this screaming, crashing, pounding music emerged, I thought of it geographically, wondering about these bands' hometowns.

From as early as I could remember I had imagined life elsewhere, or in the same place but transformed. In the first grade my teacher had read aloud to the class portions of a children's novel in French about kids who built a time machine and visited various moments in the past and future. Only one chapter of the novel made an impression on me, one where the children turned back the clock five hundred years to visit the land where their suburban homes now stood. Once there, they were amazed by the sight of green firs, frolicking deer and a wide river in place of telephone poles, driveways, roads, stop signs and parked cars. Despite the language gap, the children came across and befriended the local people who showed them around their longhouse.

This story burrowed into my six-year-old mind and I turned it into a game to play while waiting for the bus. Staring at the gradual slope of my street I would try to peer through the veil of time to see how it looked before. I knew that before the houses were built the land had been a cow pasture. But before that, hundreds of years before, I figured a verdant untouched forest must have carpeted everything and in my mind I replaced the street and its houses with trees. In my dualistic understanding of nature there was only city and forest and any stretch of grassland or treeless swamp must have been made that way by people. The world, I thought, began as a forest: a green and brown mass of trees stretching all across the globe that had slowly been cut down.

I found out about another way of looking into the past when one night my brother told me ghost stories. They were from a book designed to appear to gullible children as a credible scientific study of the paranormal. "Ghosts," my empirically minded brother explained, "are people who had a bad time in a place." He consulted the book for the scientific term. "Trauma."

"Even though they're dead, they can't leave. Their," he again referred to the book, "'psychic energy' stays around. And does stuff."

I knew, because I asked my parents repeatedly, that no one else had inhabited our house before us. So there could be no spirits of former residents locked in the walls, creaking over floorboards, opening drawers and refusing to leave the place where they had come to grief.

But there were other stories in the ghost book. Ones about Indians. At six years old what I was most afraid of was that our home was built on sacred land where Native bodies lay. I feared the possibility of living on hallowed ground, soil left in peace for centuries until disturbed by the bright yellow machines that dug our home's foundation.

Walking to school at the age of sixteen I thought of how valid my childhood fears were. Even if my house wasn't sitting atop resting bodies, I now knew that the continent of North America is one giant mass grave. Now I wished that ghosts could somehow work to undo what began five hundred years before.

In the white out I couldn't see the intersection until I walked out into it. As I squinted my eyes could barely discern the outline of the green street sign attached to the lamppost. Even though I couldn't see it I knew it read INDIAN ROAD.

[THE NIGHT ROOM]

Beneath my snow-encrusted scarf I let out a long yawn before rewinding the tape to the beginning of my favourite song.

The night before I had listened to it three times in a row, getting more jacked up with each consecutive listen. As I quietly screamed the few lyrics I could make out I played fevered air-bass on the blue rug in the centre of my bedroom floor before alternating to air-drumming

I couldn't sleep at night. Grabbing a paperback novel and climbing into the metal-framed bed I had slept on since the age of six, I would try. My hope was that reading a few pages would help my lids grow heavy, but entire chapters would fly before my eyes. Eventually I would put the novel aside in favour of listening to music on headphones and writing in my black journal. I loved the feeling of being awake while the rest of the world slumbered. Because of it I rarely got more than three hours of sleep before rising for school the next day.

My stereo, on loan from the depths of my grandfather's cellar, sat on a shelf in front of my bedroom window. Every time I pulled the needle onto another side I would look out onto the world below. The windows of nearby houses stared back at me. Under a pink winter sky the world was lit by streetlights and the lamp posts in front of each house. They burned through until dawn even though the street was empty of human movement.

Deciding to dub the record I was playing compulsively, I rummaged through a pile of cassettes on the shelf below the turntable. I tried to read the layers of scrawl on their labels. Owning only a dozen tapes, I dubbed and re-dubbed them until their magnetic ribbons grew thin and the ghost voices of the previous recording could be heard in the gaps between songs. The stickers affixed to the tapes were a dense amalgam of band names, each one written over the last. With each consecutive dubbing the inked names ceased resembling letters and words, becoming instead an illegible black mass of lines. If each thin layer of ink could be stripped away one at a time each label would provide a precise archaeology of my adolescent tastes and their constant revision.

From the heap I plucked an embarrassing relic from junior high, one of the last tapes from the days when my affinity for pop music caused me to record hours of hit songs off the top forty radio station, Energy 1200. It was during the summer following grade seven that I learned the tricks of piracy. After pushing *record* I waited with my finger on the pause button, only lifting it once the annoying DJ finished dedicating the song to a listener or announcing a contest. Once the recording was underway I waited tensely, ready to hit the stop button when an ad or station I.D. interrupted the final notes. What I didn't learn, however, was to keep track of my spoils. Without cataloguing the songs as I stole them, they were retrievable only by a long process of fast-forwarding and rewinding.

Jamming the pop-stained tape in the deck, I pressed play and record in tandem before dropping the needle lightly onto the record. There was a moment of clicking in the headphones before they filled with music.

With the buzz of punk in my ears, my path back to bed across the creaking floorboards was carelessly loud. The circuit from bed to record player that I completed over and over was only one of the paths my heavy feet travelled at night. Long past two a.m. I would often have great ideas about how to re-organize my room: lugging a filing cabinet twice my size from the basement up two flights of stairs, or making my oak desk and metal bed trade places. When not re-decorating I was either typing on my mother's old Underwood or jumping up and down in time to the music, more concerned about the record skipping than waking my sleeping family. On the occasions I went downstairs in search of food or a book my feet would often slip on the green carpeted staircase and I would crash into the table at the foot of the stair.

When these sounds reached my father's sensitive ears at the end of the hall, nine times out of ten he grumbled under his breath, rolled over and went back to sleep. But the tenth time my father would rise with a swift indignance, bursting through the tightly shut door of my bedroom.

"JESUS CHRIST! I'M TRYING TO SLEEP!" he would bark. His nighttime wardrobe was a pair of pyjama bottoms, the waistband so old and worn that he was forced to hold it with his left hand to prevent slouching in the back.

For the first few moments of his practiced dooming of my deviant sleep schedule, my father appeared to be singing along to the record playing in my headphones. When woken he possessed all the fury of a hardcore growler. His face turned a shade of crimson and, like the vocalists who fronted many of the tougher bands of the HC scene, he always performed shirtless. The illusion was broken with the concurrent unclamping of my headphones and the realization that style-obsessed hardcore front men would never wear jammies that revealed their hairy asses when they flailed about.

"I HAVE TO WORK TOMORROW! WHY DO YOU STAY UP SO LATE?" he continued, genuinely baffled.

"I don't know," I would say, trying not to laugh. "Sorry dad, I didn't mean to wake you."

It was amazing to see my dad's nocturnal transformation from a calm drinker of beer, listener of jazz and reader of the newspaper into a ball of fire.

"COULD YOU AT LEAST *TRY* TO BE QUIET WHEN I'M ASLEEP? PLEASE!" When he began pleading, the tantrum neared its end.

"I'll try to be quiet," I would lie.

With this promise dad would return to the master bedroom, exhausted from yelling. He would fall back to sleep content that he had shared the misery of being woken prematurely with everyone else in the house.

[THE WALKERS]

Marching through snow is strenuous. With each step my boot sank into a white quagmire that held my foot for a moment before letting it go. After twenty minutes of trudge I left the residential streets through a hole in the fence. Climbing down a steep incline I fell into a waist deep pile of snow. Freeing myself, I crossed the parking lot and pulled open the back door of the mall. A gust of warm air surrounded me as I stamped the snow from my boots. The lights were dim and plastic shutters hung before the gaping mouths of stores.

As I walked down the hall the swinging arms of a grey-haired man, moving at an incredible speed, nearly clipped my shoulder. At this hour the shopping centre was not open for business but used as a track by the senior citizens who lived in the condo tower across the street. Mall management encour-

aged the morning power walkers to use pedometers to track
the distance they covered each day. At the end of the month
results were tallied and the walkers told how far they would
have travelled had the distance covered been outside and in
a straight line. Magic marker script on a Bristol-board hanging near the information desk paired each walker's name with
their distance. Recent joins had only made it as far as Ottawa
Valley towns Pembroke and Bancroft, but veterans with two
or three years under their belt had already journeyed to such
exotic locales as Lima, Peru, and Baffin Island without ever
having left the Merivale Mall.

The walkers were the first of hundreds of seniors who
congregated in the mall every day, sitting on the stools of the
chain café or next to their shopping bags on the uncomfortable benches. I wasn't afraid of the aged, but was worried that
despite all the energy I put into hating my stupid suburb I
would end up spending my twilight years like them, sitting in
front of the Cotton Ginny waiting for a familiar face to walk by.

Another fast moving grey-hair in a sweat suit nearly collided with me before I removed my headphones. It was unsafe
to be hearing impaired while the sexagenarian speed freaks
circled the mall.

Exiting through a side door after crossing the concourse, I
noticed the falling snow had retreated into the low hanging
clouds. Here my daily path met Merivale Road, four lanes jostling with big box stores, mini-malls and fast food restaurants
separated by gulfs of parking and undeveloped land.

Each year when the snow melted, a local ecclesiastical
church mounted a re-enactment of the Passion of Christ. Gathering in the parking lot of the Loblaws further down Merivale,
the audience watched as a shirtless long-haired Caucasian was
crowned by a ring of plastic thorns and saddled with a cross.

The gathered crowd was usually a mélange of parishioners
and friends of the actor playing Christ. Several in attendance
were attracted by the bloody full colour posters advertising
the event. Pinned to the community billboards of local grocery stores, the images of a bloodied king of kings seemed, at

first glance, to promote a horror film.

As advertised, Christ dragged his burden along the sidewalk, past the mall and below the underpass to the parking lot of the Canadian Tire. There he was crucified and later revived to enjoy orange drink and Timbits from the makeshift breakfast buffet set up on a plastic table.

Surveying the mall's parking lot I noticed that snow plows had already pushed aside the blizzard. The morning's snow now sat piled high in the far corner of the parking lot, blocking my path to the crosswalk and my school on the other side of the road. Approaching the mountain of snow, I pulled off my left mitten and read my watch. Realizing I was already late, my pace slowed; no point in hurrying now.

From my pocket I grabbed my walkman and flipped the tape. The air was growing frigid without the insulation of snowfall and as I pressed the play button I wasn't surprised that the cold was sapping the batteries. The music slowed to a speed that rendered the song unrecognizable, but I left it on anyway.

As I climbed the freshly erected precipice of snow, the now lugubrious voice of a young Ian MacKaye encouraged me on. "IIII ccccaaaannnn'tttt kkkkeeeeeeeepppp uuuupppp / ooo-ouuuutttt oooffff sssstttteepppp wwwwiiiittttth tttthhhheeee wwwwooooorrrrlllldddd!!!!"

[LEGALIZE IT]
Twenty minutes before homeroom and following at five minute intervals, the bell warned the students marching from buses to their lockers that the school day was creeping ever closer. When the final bell signalled the beginning of home-room the hallways emptied, locker doors slammed and shoes squeaked across the waxed floor.

The bell made a sound similar to two buttons on a touch tone phone being pushed in quick succession. This bullying sound rigidly maintained the schedule each student received on the first day of school

Homeroom was but a tiny sliver at the top of that schedule. Consisting of attendance, the ritual standing for "O Canada," and the morning announcements chirped over the P.A. by the student body's highest elected representatives, the poorly named and eternally perky Head Boy and Head Girl, it was all over in ten minutes. I was glad to have missed it as I waited in the long line of students signing in late in the school's office.

"It's Miller, isn't it?" one of the secretaries asked me. "It says here this morning was your eighth late since the Christmas break." After accruing ten lates in a semester a detention was handed out. I was playing it pretty close to the line.

"I had to climb a mountain of snow to get here!" I said, in a fake cheery voice, before she handed me a late slip. "Fucking asshole," I muttered as I pulled the office door behind me.

This was the year I finally gave up on high school. After what happened in the fall I had withdrawn any involvement in the official life of school. No more assemblies, dances, plays or watching football. Definitely no more clubs. Now I knew that school was nothing but a game to be played. Nothing more than classes and report cards.

Although not previously a beacon of school spirit, I had engaged in activities sanctioned by the administration during my first two years of high school. My pimply visage had appeared more than once in the group photographs found in the 'clubs' section of the yearbook.

My first flirtation with the official extra-curricular scene occurred two years before when my brother convinced me to join the debating team. He had argued at several tournaments held on southern Ontario university campuses and was billetted in dorms. As a result he was convinced that it was a good way to see the world. The bulk of his teammates had graduated the summer before and the squad was desperate for fresh blood. Starting a membership drive, my brother drafted me and a few of my friends.

The first meeting was held in a classroom during lunch one early September day. In the first practice debate I was pitted against Eric, who lived in my neighbourhood and against whom I was forced to argue for the continued prohibition of the psychedelic drug known colloquially as 'pot.' Eric had the unfair advantage of a subscription to *High Times* magazine and a history of using said psychedelic that I did not.

"It would be good for the economy," Eric argued in favour of legalization. "Just think of all the money that could be made from selling hemp rope and clothes. And studies show that pot has," he stared off into space for a moment, "...uh, incredible health benefits for its users."

"But..." thirty seconds into debate I was already stymied. "What about, uh... families?" I asked, unsure of what my question meant. My brother watched attentively, eating his sandwich at a nearby desk.

"Think of how many families are destroyed by the current *draconian*," Eric smiled, remembering the word from an opinion piece in his favourite magazine, "draconian measures the government takes against drug dealers. Some people go to jail for up to fifty years. *That* tears apart families."

Eric was more informed on the subject and thus I deferred to his point of view.

"Okay, well... legalize it." I said.

"Thanks," Eric said. "I will."

"There's still a minute left on the clock! You have to keep arguing!" My brother spoke frantically, pointing at his watch. Bits of tuna salad stuck in his braces were revealed as he attempted to coach us on the most basic tenet of debate. "Never concede to your opponent!"

"But he convinced me."

"It doesn't matter, you gotta keep going!"

"I don't want to," I said, stubbornly.

After abandoning the debating team I wrote news pieces for the student newspaper, but when they published my poorly informed yet passionate article about Indonesia's illegal twenty year occupation of East Timor, whole paragraphs were missing and I left my position as International Correspondent in a huff.

When I entered grade eleven that fall it followed a summer of attending hardcore shows. I thought being a punk would somehow disqualify me from the universe of school clubs and activities. Unfortunately that year marked my most intense involvement with a club yet. One which, of course, ended in disaster.

Walking to my locker I passed Mr. Michel's classroom, catching a glimpse of him through a small window set into the door. Things were different between us now, but I didn't have time to worry about it as I continued down the empty hall.

(2004-07, previously unpublished)

THE SOCIAL JUSTICE CLUB
Part Two: Recruits

[ORIGIN]

TWO WEEKS INTO THE SCHOOL YEAR I WAS BOLTING DOWN THE hall, late to class again and feeling bad about it. The year before I had failed three of my ten classes. Two of those, Math and Computers, were not difficult to explain to my mom. She was sympathetic to my poor grasp of numbers.

But this went beyond just numbers. "Writer's Craft?" she had asked beguiled, when she perused my report card. "How the hell did you fail Writer's Craft? All you ever do is fill up that notebook of yours." I hung my head in shame.

After nearly burning a hole in my forehead with concentration I actually passed Grade Ten Math in summer school with a solid B. That victory, coupled with the many hours of labour volunteered to my grandmother's overgrown half-acre garden, set me on the path of redemption. Now that I was back in school I was actually going to *try*. For my mother's sake. But first I needed to get to class on time.

The bell rang as I rounded a corner. I broke into a full sprint.

"Jeff," Mr. Michel said, sticking his head out of a classroom door.

"Okay. No running in the halls." I replied, slowing my pace to a speedy walk.

"Can I talk to you?" he called after me.

"Sure. When?" I asked without looking back. What could he possibly have to talk to me about anyway? He wasn't teaching any of my classes this year.

"Now."

I turned to face him for the first time since our exchange began, talking to him from halfway down the corridor. "But, but..." I pointed to the ceiling, attempting to signify the bell that rang a minute before.

"I'll write you a note."

He had me. Notes from teachers offered a rare window of time that couldn't be tracked. I never used them to do anything devious, I just enjoyed walking to class slowly down the empty hallways and taking some extra time at the water fountain.

"You're not teaching this period?" I asked, as I passed through the door of his classroom. The tall window of the far wall framed a sky freighted with the high clouds of late summer.

"No, it's my spare period. I've got a hundred quizzes to mark. Lucky me." he said, picking up the thick pile of paper from his desk and fanning himself.

While the school's other English teachers were all hairless faces and drab sweaters, Mr. Michel wore a well-groomed goatee and a multi-coloured vest. Despite his unorthodox wardrobe he was an English teacher at heart, as evidenced by his penchant for long digressions. The most memorable of these occurred one day the year before, when his instruction of *Macbeth* veered into a prolonged explanation of the tape worm that his intestinal tract hosted when he lived in South America and how he rid himself of it.

"Ten minutes after I took the anti-worm pill it felt like there was a bomb going off in my stomach," he said. "I had to run to the toilet, and when it came out—"

He stopped mid-sentence and said "I shouldn't really be telling you guys this," a tacit reminder that what he was about to divulge did not fall within the provincial education guidelines and, as such, could never leave the room. A chorus of

"C'mon!" and "We won't tell!" from my classmates prompted him to continue.

"It came out in three big pieces," he said finally, stretching his arms as far as he could to demonstrate the lengths of parasite. "And it came out fast."

"At the last school I taught at we had an environmental club," he began as I sat down in front of his desk.

"Uh huh." I wondered what he was getting at.

Most teachers at my high school were old guard and as they closed in on retirement they had less optimism with each passing minute. Mr. Michel, however, was still young enough to hope. Every year on the first day of class he prepared an elaborate blackboard message encouraging students to buy post-consumer notebooks and loose leaf, including directions to the stationer that sold recycled paper downtown. If he was disappointed when students arrived the next day with reams of paper made from virgin clear-cut purchased at the big box office supply store he didn't show it.

"That club went really well. We got the school to double its paper recycling in just one year! Above even our targets!" He paused to let the numbers sink in. "Now, I know school participation isn't really as high here as at my last school."

Despite the wide variety of clubs offered by at Merivale High, smoking dope behind the arena and playing "Come As You Are" on acoustic guitar were still the most popular lunchtime pursuits. Fighting and/or watching a fight in the parking lot came in a close third.

"I read the political articles you and your friends wrote in the school newspaper last year and I think we could do some good stuff if we started a social advocacy club here. We could take on some human rights issues and raise money and awareness." Noticing me nodding, he took this as an affirmative to his proposal. "You think so? Great!"

"But I—" I tried to explain that I was actually just agreeing with his earlier comment about the lack of school spirit but he cut me off.

"Why don't you tell your friends about it and next Thursday

at lunch we'll have a meeting here in my classroom. Okay," he said, smiling as he handed me my note. "See you later!" He grabbed a quiz from the top of the pile and began marking it with a red pen. I sat across from him for a moment, but he refused to look up from his work.

I stumbled out into the hallway wondering what I had gotten myself into.

[THE NON-COMPETITIVE LEAGUE]
Near the end of lunch that day I saw my first potential recruit. I was walking down the hall when I noticed a charged-up green mohawk emerging from one of the school's more secluded bathrooms. The sleeves of the mohican's jean jacket were skillfully removed and as he turned down the hall the lyrics to a Crass song transcribed in liquid paper across his back were clearly visible. The band's logo, by far the most geometrically complex of any punk band, was painted above the lyrics.

An assortment of spikes and silkscreened patches also adorned the vest. One held the image of a giant fist punching a fractured swastika while another read "Fur is Dead" over a grainy black and white image of what I could only guess was a mink pelt. The vested punk's face was a constellation of acne covered by the long blonde whiskers he considered a beard. I called his name and as he approached I saw his mouth was drawn into a sneer. I had heard the rumours, but hadn't believed them. After being expelled for the third, and many thought final, time the summer before, Alex had somehow been re-admitted to Merivale High School.

I first met Alex in grade nine when we were both sentenced to the same obligatory gym class. It was taught by Mr. Nugent, a jolly imp of a man standing no more than five feet tall. Each morning he walked across the gymnasium dressed in shorts and a t-shirt singing to himself, "Born Free / free as the grass grows." He alternated between crooning and whistling the melody of his personal theme song.

Dwarfed by many of his post-pubescent students, 'the Nuge' was genuinely excited and *happy* to be a physical educator.

He had no sadistic aims to whip us into peak physical shape comparable to a squadron of Hitler Youth. Instead his mission was the promotion of physical fitness through a series of team sports, with a strong emphasis on fun.

Despite this noble goal, after the first month of teaching our class he witnessed a disturbing trend. The class was evenly split between jock and spazz and as such often degenerated into a desperate blood sport of the latter running from the former across the football field.

Early in October the Nuge gathered the class into a semi-circle on the waxed wood planks of the gymnasium floor. He sat on a red rubber ball, a whistle hanging around his neck. "I've decided to divide the class into two leagues," he said soberly. "The first will be for the guys who really take sports seriously and want to play hard—" Here his speech was interrupted by the howls and high-fives of ravenous jocks.

"The other league is for the..." he paused to consider his words.

"Geeks?" a jock muttered to a crony, loud enough to be heard and ignored.

"For the guys who just want to have fun!" was how we, the blossoming freaks with matchstick limbs, were dubbed by our miniature teacher.

If someone had had the foresight to document the games played by the Non-Competitive League over the remainder of the year it would have provided fodder for the ultimate sports bloopers video. In our quest to 'just have fun' we committed a truly awesome array of crimes against sport, be they foul balls, errors, off-sides or just a profound inability to throw a football. Without the pressure of playing with the task-oriented jocks, we let it all hang out. On the field or in the gym we were safe, protected by the patron saint of freaks, a gym teacher who had the benevolence to segregate.

We ignored each other in the halls between classes, each of us ashamed of our profound collective failure as athletes. When we did acknowledge each other with a nod, real communication was avoided as we each considered ourselves higher on the social ladder than the other.

In the intricately ordered, nearly lupine hierarchy of grade nine gym class, none were lower on the totem pole than Alex, the future punk. He simply refused to adopt a strategy to avoid the jocks' derision. The extra large *Star Trek* t-shirts hanging from his spindly frame instantly called attention to his Omega status. Despite this, Alex stood tall, he was a geek and somehow *proud* of it. He didn't speak often, but when he did it was without any sense of embarrassment for what he was.

The joy, or at least lack of shame, he took in his position as gym class *untermensch* drove the jocks insane. In the games of dodgeball played before the class was partitioned, Alex was often at the epicenter of the opposing team's volleys. During one such game he was struck just below the clinging waistband of his jogging pants.

In an unwritten rule of gym class, being hit below the belt was an event that called for a certain dramatic flair. If a ball in flight struck anywhere within thirty centimetres of your genitals it was expected of you to writhe on the floor, emitting moans approximating a death rattle. Even the writing of a will on the gym floor was not uncommon. This is because at the age of fourteen your balls are obviously so *big* and so *fragile* that you could *die* if they were somehow broken in gym class.

While a chorus of jocks let out a howl of "OOHH!" at their classmate's suffering, Alex refused to pretend to be in pain when he wasn't. He shrugged off his groin hit, bending forward and taking a breath before standing straight and resuming play.

"That ain't right," one of the jocks said, shaking his head in disbelief.

At the end of grade nine the Non-Competitive League disbanded. A year later, all of its former members were punks, Alex being the first and the de facto leader. Before anyone else had the guts to shave their head Alex already had a charged hawk, a customized jean jacket, and wore a dog collar he shoplifted from the pet store at the mall. He had also been soundly beaten by the jocks of the higher grades for these reasons more than once. As a punk he refined his gym class aloofness into an extreme cool. When hockey-haired boneheads called him "faggot" he'd look right through them. Or worse, he'd smile. That *really* pissed them off.

One day he took me to his locker. The inside of its door was decorated with anti-police propaganda and photos of Rancid cut from *Details* magazine. "I know they're sell-outs," he said of the million-selling Berkeley pop punk band, "but when I put these pictures up this girl who has the locker next to me said 'Ew, they're *so* ugly,' so I left them up just to fuck with her." He looked like a rat when he smiled. "Fuck pretty people. I *like* ugly."

"How did you get back into school?" I asked, stunned to see him, and yet somehow not surprised.

"Well, it took a couple weeks, but I finally had a meeting with my mom and Baird," he sneered when he mentioned the name of the hated vice-principal.

He twisted his voice so that it had a saccharine quality, "I told them I'd try really, really hard this year." He blew air through his teeth and snarled "Fuck it."

"Well, lunch is over. I got Biology but I fuckin' hate it. I'm skipping to meet Tops at Rockwell's." The punks loved hanging out in the mall's family restaurant, named after the painter who invented the suburban pastoral. They equally enjoyed the free refills and the shocked looks of the blue-haired grannies who were the restaurant's only other afternoon clientele. Basking in the scowls, they paid for their drinks in mountains of dimes and pennies, stiffing on the tip every time.

Before he left I told him of Thursday's inaugural meeting of Mr. Michel's club. A raspy "Maybe," was the closest he would come to confirming his appearance.

As Alex walked down the hall to the door, I saw a new addition to his black jean vest. Another silkscreened patch, this one was located just below the Crass lyrics. It read "I HATE JOCKS."

[ENCLAVES]

The true business of high school occurs at lunch. After a morning of being driven from one class to the next, the unstructured forty-five minutes that the administration had the nerve to call lunch 'hour' was a panacea.

Fights were fought, drugs dealt, games of asshole played, french fries from the cafetorium consumed, and the parking lot lined with students marching to the mall, going home or smoking cigarettes. At lunch most of the freaks chose to sequester themselves in the school's more protected alcoves.

Those with gothic tendencies, which, as far as I could tell, consisted of occasionally wearing black, reading thousand-plus-page Victorian novels, and drawing little black curlicues next to their eyes in tribute to some Egyptian death goddess, chose to ensconce themselves in a sunny hallway by the art room.

Those with aspirations to be punk stationed themselves in front of my locker in hallway D. Most were also interested in metal, despite Alex feeding them a strict diet of the canonical works of DK, OP IV, and Crass.

It was Monday and I was trying to convince the ten or so boys congregated around my locker to come to the first meeting of Mr. Michel's club. As with the goths, whom I had petitioned the Friday before, I received only a tepid response.

Tops grunted and pulled a Sepultura tape from his pocket, jamming it into the tiny ghetto blaster. The harshness of Brazilian thrash was the musical equivalent of the chemical burn of his daily lunch: bright yellow onion-flavoured rings chased by a litre bottle of generic cola, both purchased from the dollar store in the mall.

The small tape player was plugged into one of the wall jacks that were in every hall of the school. This availability of electricity had prompted Alex, in the few days since his return, to commandeer an empty locker nearby. Now it held a coffee maker saved from the trash, a can of ground beans and a box of filters. Jacked in, the machine brewed a cup in three minutes and a pot in ten. The lock's combination was widely circulated and the door to the coffee locker swung open at least a half dozen times a day.

Some who hung out everyday at lunch weren't into punk *or* metal, which sometimes caused difficulties. As the abrasive riffs poured forth from the ghetto blaster, Beamish stood up and said, "Man, I'm sick of this shit. Why don't we ever listen to my Archies tape, huh? Or we could tune into Oldies 94.5 ?"

"No hippie shit!" Alex sneered authoritatively.

"I'm not a hippie, man," Beamish said, pushing his floppy hair out of his eyes. "I just like a melody every now and then. I'm sick of always listening to the same three fucking metal tapes. Christ!"

Chris, a recent transfer from another school with long hair that was black, except for the skunk-like blonde stripe on the top of his head, spoke up sheepishly. "I've got Amebix? Nail-bomb? Bolt Thrower?"

"Fuck you guys," Beamish dismissed Chris's help. "I'm going for a smoke."

"Oh come on, Nailbomb have some incredibly melodic parts!"

Among those who rebelled most against rebellion was Mikey Thomas, a self-described 'cowboy' from 'the sticks' who for some reason hung out with us every day. He wore cowboy boots and a white straw Stetson when it got hot. When the ghetto blaster was off, he played "Ocean Front Property" on his acoustic guitar, singing to us in a clear voice. One day he showed up to school with his lasso, to show us punks how good he was getting at roping steer. Instead, we tied him up and six of us dragged him at incredible speed down the freshly waxed hallway of the school's second floor. His screams turned to laughter as he began to enjoy the ride, until we approached a stairway. "Not down the stairs! Don't drag me down the stairs!" he yelled, before a teacher stopped us.

"Wait, Beamish, I'll go with you!" I called after him down the hall. Having already visited both freak enclaves to recruit for the club, I now set out to tell others. I sought those who didn't want to be affiliated with either group, choosing instead to spend lunch walking the halls, hiding in the library or disappearing entirely.

[SUNDAR]

"Sounds good," Sundar said after I told him about the club. "We should raise money for Northern Cree land claims disputes." He was skinny, wore shoulder length hair, glasses, and spoke in a manner that was serious, but offered occasional glimpses of hilarity. Once he told me that he was so into heavy metal as a kid that when he heard there was a song called "Twist and Shout" he immediately assumed it must be about torture.

We had met only a week before, when I heard a voice behind me ask "Were you at Fugazi last night?" Turning to see who spoke, I saw a spindly twelfth grader dressed in well-worn jeans and a button-up shirt.

In the days after rock concerts the school's hallways were always peppered with people wearing identical oversized band t-shirts. Sometimes it was jocks with earth-tone shirts bearing the name of Can Rock superstars The Tragically Hip. Other days it was headbangers whose black shirts were adorned with images of carnage and unreadable logos. These shirts were not only souvenirs but also a way of seeking out kindred spirits.

Fugazi didn't sell any such identity defining clothing, or anything, at their shows. Instead, they had written a song about the evils of hawking rock souvenirs. After being weaned on intense merchandising as a child, when cartoon shows were also toys, a pair of pyjamas, a colouring book and a fast food meal, I now agreed with Fugazi's stance against graven images. It was incredibly righteous to be sure, but the fallout was that without t-shirts there was no way of knowing who your allies were. That is, unless, like Sundar, you spied a fellow student and then talked to him at school the next day.

"Weren't they so... fucking... awesome?" he accentuated each word by jerkily flinging his forearms up and down. As with his first question, my response was a nod. He looked as if he was about to spontaneously combust.

In the few minutes we talked he told me that he lived in Barrhaven, a far-off suburb, and that he played guitar. We swapped the names of the records we owned and vowed to tape them for each other.

"Shotmaker RULED!" he said of the opening band. "That was the first time I saw them."

"I was at their record release show in May at 5 Arlington. It cost seven bucks. *And,*" I delivered the clincher, "the LP came free with the show."

My motivation was not, I swear, to come off as cool. I would have been the first to admit that I didn't know anyone in 'the scene.' No, instead of coming off like an insider I was as awed as Sundar when I repeated "Seven bucks for a show and a record." The words weaved magic about us both.

"Awesome," Sundar whispered, as if to himself, as he shook his head. "Fucking awesome." And it was.

I had found someone at school who understood that punk had progressed beyond the bands on Alex's patched vest, which had all come and gone almost a decade before. What was happening was happening now, and if it wasn't in the suburbs it wasn't that far away; it was getting closer by the day.

"I'll see you Thursday," Sundar said gravely, clamping the lid on his re-sealable sandwich container and throwing it into his open locker.

[MATTEO]

"I went door to door campaigning around here, and Jesus, it was just so fucking disgusting," Matteo said. He had volunteered for the NDP during the provincial election in June and every day when we walked the path through the rowhouses behind the mall he railed against their inhabitants' political leanings.

"I told them all the programs we were campaigning for. More money for welfare. Taxing the rich to pay for the poor. *Whatever.* Then after my whole spiel they'd tell me they were voting for Harris!" We sneered in unison at the mention of the Conservative premier, "Because he was giving a hundred dollar tax refund to *everyone*, even the fucking richest people!

"God, I hate being such a bleeding heart liberal. Having to fight for these poor morons... " He was incensed, but I took issue with his classism.

"Whoa, whoa."

"I know, I know, I might as well be a fucking Tory for all the shit I say about poor people. But it's true."

Matteo had never been afraid to say what he felt. We met in junior high school when I was an unpopular eighth grader and he was in the grade below. The school we attended consisted solely of these two grades, so that by the time a student reached the senior year, interacting with those a year below you was severely frowned upon.

As a loser, the highly policed lines between grades did not apply to me, so I didn't push Matteo from the black vinyl bus seat onto the floor that first day he sat next to me.

"I watched *The Boys of St. Vincent* last night," was the first thing he ever said to me. I wondered if he was attempting sophistication by mentioning the controversial CBC mini-series about buggery at a Catholic Newfoundland boarding school.

"I though it would be sexy, I mean, *hello*, the guy who plays that priest is *hot*. But really it was just fucking boring," he said. "Jesus Christ, where were the sex scenes?"

For a moment I stared at the skinny preppy sitting beside me in total shock, my mouth agape. Then I began laughing hysterically. Matteo's sense of humour, despite our crucial disparity in age, was far more sardonic than the typical *Saturday Night Live* re-hashes my fellow numbskull eighth graders were engaged in.

"Monsieur G. is *such* a fag," he said the next day, as the bus weaved its way through the suburban streets, "and Mademoiselle M. is a total dyke. Obviously." He used 'fag' and 'dyke' in a way that was somehow different than the way my idiot friends used them.

Everything Matteo told me on our morning bus rides to school, like that some teachers might not be straight, were things I had never thought of before. He opened my eyes to a world that existed right below the surface of the everyday, a secret knowledge there to discover, if you cared to look.

It only dawned on me that *he* was gay months later. After I figured it out I set aside some time to try to think about how his homosexuality made me feel. I hadn't even had my first

wet dream and didn't know what sex really was, so I found it
difficult to form an opinion. The main shocker was that he was
sexual. From watching television I knew there were no indif-
ferent opinions on the subject so, in the end, I figured I was
probably homophobic. I tried to think about it some more,
but was distracted by one of the comic books on my bedroom
floor. The next day Matteo and I rode the bus together as usual.

Later, in high school, we walked home from school together almost every day, usually catching up with each other
by the hole in the fence that led to the rowhouses from the
mall parking lot.

Of the hundreds of conversations we had while walking together I only remember a few, and they're hazy in my memory.
Once he told me about attending a convention of the youth
wing of the NDP in a hotel downtown. After discovering that
the Liberal youth conference was occurring a few stories below,
he and his fellow delegates ordered buckets of fried chicken and
attacked the adolescent Whigs with volleys of wings and thighs.

Another story involving thighs included D., who starred in
Merivale's production of *The Wiz*. One spring night he and
Matteo were caught fucking in the back seat of his parents' car
in the Toys R Us parking lot.

"I was on top when the cop knocked on the window. He had
his flashlight on and said 'Can we see your girlfriend's face?'
When he saw D. his whole attitude changed.

"He was like 'Oh...' for a minute, but then said 'Don't worry.
You just need to move the car out of the parking lot. You can't
really do this here. I'm not going to tell your parents or anything.' And then he just let us go."

"Huh."

"Yeah, you could tell *he'd* had his sensitivity training." Matteo
let out a loud "HA!" He actually said ha when he laughed.

"I can't be in your club." Matteo said. It was Tuesday and I was
starting to worry if anyone would be at the meeting. "I'm
sorry, I've got track and field practice on Thursday. You know
I can't say no to a locker room full of hot teenage boys!" he

smacked his lips. "Mmm."

"It's all about sleep-overs," he had once told me, elaborating on his modus operandi for sexual adventures. "You'd be surprised what you can get a horny fifteen-year-old 'straight boy'" he air quoted, "to do. Mamma mia!"

"I'm so excited about the Madonna 'Egos and Icons' tonight!" he said, changing the subject. Matteo's fandom for The Queen of Pop was lifelong and deep. The previous summer he had gone to a fan convention held at a motel in the Detroit suburb the diva grew up in. Admission included a bus tour past the Ciccone family home.

Even after I went punk and refused to listen to even Green Day because they were sell-outs I gleefully accepted the glamorous Madonna CDs Matteo foisted on me. That they came from Matteo somehow made it okay. "Ugh, why do you listen to that *ugly* music," he had asked once when I put my walkman headphones on his ears.

"God, I hope my grandma isn't watching porn when I get home," he complained. "She orders pay-per-view porno movies and then denies ever watching them and tries to blame *me* for ordering them when the bill comes," he ranted. "I just wanna be like, listen grandma, I'm a *fag*. I'm not ordering straight porn from fucking pay-per-view."

We arrived in front of his family's large home, the exterior covered in white stone. Matteo kissed me on both cheeks, making an exaggerated "MWAH" sound as he did so.

"Don't forget to watch the Madonna special on Much Music tonight!" he called after me.

[OMAR]

Walking down the hall the day before the meeting, I saw the one person I hadn't yet tried to recruit for the club. Leaning against a wall in the school foyer he was holding court, surrounded by his dour-looking homeboys and four giggling girls.

I waved and in a minute he came over to talk to me.

"Jeff man! What's happening?"

I told him, but he had to decline. "United Colours of Merivale meets tomorrow at lunch, yo," he came in close and whispered in my ear. "We're doing a fashion show this year. You should get in on this club, it's where all the fly honeys are at!"

"Damn," I said.

"You know!" he slapped my back. "That's my boy-ee!"

Tipping the scales at well over two hundred and fifty pounds and with a face of acne and wire rim glasses, one would think Omar would have some major liabilities in the universe of teen popularity. Despite these potential setbacks he played on the football team and was always sweet-talking young ladies.

He was born in Bethlehem ("Like Jesus!" he'd say with a smile) but always identified himself as Lebanese. While the school's large pan-Arabic student body were referred to by the racial epithet "Leb" by their detractors, Omar spun the term around, often proclaiming "I'm Leb and proud!" in conversation.

He made teachers uneasy. Some believed him to be the kingpin of a Lebanese gang, but I never thought that he could be into any dirty business.

But there was that one day at lunch when I saw him looking upset in the hall and asked him what the matter was. His reply was "There's this rumour that me and some of my boys are going to roll up on Laurentian High in a white minivan with some gats to take out some suckas."

I mumbled my condolences, unsure of what to say. High school is the centre of the most scurrilous libel. Someone can joke about having a water gun and wanting to spray a teacher at lunch and the next thing the cops are breaking open his locker. Broken telephone is some dangerous shit.

"Yo! I *know*. A white minivan? Who the fuck do they think I am? I ain't driving no *white* minivan." He shook his head and then said "I gotta get outta here!"

I met Omar in Drama class the year before. On the first day we played a game where a student picked a famous person and then everyone else had to ask questions and guess who it was. Omar's celebrity pick stymied the class until we eventually gave up. "Who is it, Omar?" Mrs. Ruby asked.

With his trademark wide smile, Omar said, "It's my hero, missus. Biggie Smalls, the Notorious B. I. G.!"

While the class argued that they had never heard of Bed-Stuy's finest, whose first album had only just been released, one of Omar's friends called "BUP BUP!" in appreciation.

His friends wore their shirts tucked in and hair slicked back. None of them understood why he associated with a freak such as me. Despite this, Omar was positively giddy whenever he saw me and I was glad to be in his good graces. His connections had come in handy back in the earliest reaches of high school, during my brief career as a brawler. One day at lunch I was sitting in the gym bleachers watching intramural basketball when, from behind, my toque was grabbed from my head.

"Hey!" I swivelled. I had never seen the person behind me before. "Give me my hat back."

"What hat?" he said, having somehow hidden my toque.

High school was shot through with such incidents, random acts of unkindness. The antagonism at the hands of absolute strangers for no reason is something I've yet to understand.

"Give me my hat back," I repeated and he again countered with "What hat?"

Who pushed first in my first and last fight is lost to the sands of time. My battle was minor league compared to the marquee fights that happened out in the parking lot at lunch or after school. Those fights were instantly surrounded by jostling spectators that formed into a tight circle. All that passers-by could see was a wide crowd crammed together, all wearing jackets with sports team logos across the back.

Whenever I saw a big fight I walked in the opposite direction. The howls and chants carried on the wind after me. I felt if I tried to catch a glimpse of the beat-down I would be sucked to the centre of the vortex. My voyeurism would implicate me in the violence and I would be forced to fend off punches from a larger opponent, while trying to avoid the sharp jabs and kicks from the first row of spectators.

After pushing each other, our fight was broken up a minute

later by the gym supervisor.

"I saw what happened." Suddenly Omar was at my side. "This is bullshit what they're doing to you! That motherfucker started it!" After consoling me he gave his eyewitness account to the teacher in an attempt to exonerate me.

Under the school's zero tolerance policy on violence the punishment for fighting was a one day 'in school' suspension. Two weeks after the fight I was paired with another miscreant and forced to rake leaves. Another task was collecting garbage from bins and taking it to a dumpster, something that proved a harbinger for my working life, which has often consisted of moving garbage from small to large receptacles.

I wonder how they got this by the janitors' union. I imagine the negotiations went as such:

Carleton School Board: So we figure that your job is really worthless and so inherently demeaning that we're going make bad kids do it in order to humiliate them and potentially scare them straight, and if not, they'll learn vital skills in a terrible profession which might keep them out of the criminal class.

Janitors' Union: Well...

Carleton School Board: Okay, great!

While I mopped the cafetorium floor that day, Omar approached me and whispered "If you hear anything about there being a hit on you from the Mexicans, don't worry. If anyone touches you they're going to have to deal with the Lebs, okay? I told 'em that."

The previously cheery Omar was gone and the boy in front of my mop was strictly business. He tensed his right hand into a fist and I did the same, meekly touching mine to his.

"A'ight," he said. "I'm going to get some fries, I'll see you later on."

It was Wednesday afternoon and Omar was a long shot and the last person on my list of potential recruits. With his rebuff I mentally prepared myself for a meeting the next day that involved me sitting awkwardly in an empty classroom with Mr. Michel.

(Ghost Pine #10: Wires, 2006)

THE FIRST MEETING OF THE SOCIAL JUSTICE CLUB

I ATE MY BAG LUNCH IN THREE MINUTES FLAT, STARING AT THE hands of the clock. Nothing happened. Mr. Michel sat at his desk leafing through the newspaper. He unscrewed the top of his thermos and poured soup into a mug.

"I told everybody," I confessed.

"Sure," he said casually.

"Everybody."

He only acknowledged the empty classroom a few minutes later, looking up from his paper and joking nonchalantly "Pretty small club, eh?"

I nodded and managed a small smile, but "Fuck you" was what I was thinking. My brain whirred with despair. After all the running around I did to start this club, it's not my fault that no one showed up, I thought. That's what I get for getting involved with this shit.

Yes. Fuck extra-curriculars, fuck high school, and fuck me for a being fool enough to believe, in my most optimistic moments, that my fellow students could be united into the vanguard of a suburban revolutionary congress. No one was coming. Fuck.

Then Sundar walked in. His shoulder length curls bobbed as he greeted me. "Uh, hi," he said.

"No one's here," I said. "No one's coming." If people hadn't come in the first ten minutes of lunch break I figured they were obviously never going to come. I was ready to throw in the towel and go back to sitting in front of my locker, being laughed at by my friends.

But the sun was out. Maybe I would walk out past the football field, instead. Slipping through the gate that opened onto the soccer fields next to the industrial park I could sit there in silence, stare at the clouds and wonder yet again how the fuck I was going to survive two and a half more years of high school.

"I just talked to some people in the hall. They said they were coming. People are coming," Sundar said, completely sure.

He sat down at the desk next to mine and pulled a package of sesame snaps from his pocket, offering me one after he tore open the plastic.

Each minute following brought a few people through the classroom door, and then more, until groups of four and five were clamouring for the few remaining seats. Some sat on the floor while others stood or leaned against the walls. The room filled with the great excited chatter of people arriving on the threshold of something unknown together. We chatted as if attending some teen cocktail hour and all the while people I hadn't told about the meeting arrived with others I had never even seen before. The ugly room that housed hours of sedate pedagogy was alive in a way I never imagined it could be.

Oh, and then the goths arrived. The goths! Really. I hardly knew them, but had guessed that their wardrobe of nihilism and black eyeliner was just a costume. They arrived in black capes of gloom and pants stitched with graveyard mist, but I knew with their arrival that they loved, not hated, the world.

The room twittered with the excitement of individuals realizing that maybe, unexpectedly—although they had hoped, always hoped—they had found a fellowship, a step above a gang, mightier than a clique. And into all of this joy came the punks, dark clouds tied to their mohawks. They sat in the aisles between desks, crossing their legs like oversized kindergartners. Alex stood next to me in front of the blackboard, detailing his latest encounter with the school administration, only to be interrupted by a throat-clearing that cut through the room's conversations.

"It's twenty past," Mr. Michel said. "I think you'd better get started."

"Okay." I said. And then, all confidence suddenly drained, asked "How do we do that?"

"However you want. It's your guys's club, I'm just the supervisor."

"Uh," I said. As much work as I had put into recruiting, I never for a moment considered what I would say if people actually showed up at the meeting.

"Okay," I said, "Welcome to the first meeting of the Social Justice Club."

"Yeah, *welcome*," Alex parroted.

"We're all here because we believe that the world is a pretty messed up place. The idea behind this club, I guess, is that we can somehow make a difference for the better.

"So to begin, I guess I would just like to know what, uh, everyone is interested in working on..." I was overwhelmed. "There are a lot of issues, but I think we should work on the ones that we can all agree on. A democracy..."

"So call 'em out and we'll write them down on the board," Alex said, handing me some chalk.

"Okay, I'll write down a political issue I'm concerned about for a start." I brushed off the remnants of white from the board and then wrote 'East Timor,' the nation illegally occupied by Indonesia, on the board in the clearest script I could manage.

As I wrote the 'i' of Timor Sundar suggested we look into Native land claims and before I had enough time to write that out in full someone else called out "Vegetarianism," and so it went. After five minutes of writing on the black board, the suggestions slowly came to an end. My hand was cramped and the board was covered with problems. Stepping back and looking at all the white chalk lines, I was amazed at the breadth of our grievances. Every problem we could think of was up there, an alphabet of dissent from Animal Rights to Women's Issues.

"Okay," I said. I took a deep breath, letting it sink it. The world was fucked. "Maybe we could divide into small groups that work on an issue that's important to us. Then each committee can bring their ideas to the rest of the club and we can talk about what to do. And then we'll do it."

Desks creaked as they merged into clumps of three or four, small islands of talk.

In fifteen minutes Sundar had already planned our first action, brought it to the group and had it approved unanimously. In fourteen days we were going to sell fair trade coffee and chocolate in the foyer.

We were running out of time. As the electronic bell sounded, final questions were asked.

"Can we be on more than one committee?"

"Yes!" Alex called.

"Do we need a leader?"

"No! We're Anarchists!" he pronounced.

Mr. Michel looked up from his from his paper, having sat in disinterested silence for the last half hour. "Oh, that reminds me, you need to elect two leaders to represent you."

Alex sneered.

"It's policy," Mr. Michel shrugged.

"I nominate Jeff," Sundar called.

"Alex!" a voice called.

I wrote both Alex's and my name in the small space on the board that wasn't covered in scrawl. "Okay, who else?" I asked, prepared for a deluge similar to our rapid diagnosis of the world's ills.

The class was silent. I looked to Sundar; he was probably the smartest person in the room, but he was staring out the window, suddenly entranced by the birds flitting outside.

"Well, I guess we don't need to have a vote," Mr. Michel said, wrapping things up. "Congratulations to club presidents Alex and Jeff!"

"Co-coordinators, maybe?" I suggested, uncomfortable with my new title.

"Four more years! Four more years!" Alex yelled, holding his arms over his head in celebration. The punks howled their approval. Alex ran to Tops, his right arm outstretched for a high five. Instead of congratulating his friend, Tops simply picked him up, hung him over his shoulder and carried him out of the room.

(Ghost Pine #11: Crows, 2007)

THE SOCIAL JUSTICE CLUB
Part Three

I.

SUNDAR WAS WAITING FOR ME BY THE RUSTED BIKE RACKS IN front of the school, his breath rising into the pale sky.

"Is that the—?" Sundar looked around cautiously; even if there was no one else around our plan was secret. "Is that the *thing?*" He pointed at the six foot tall white cylinder I had carried to school.

I nodded and discreetly handed him a canvas bag. He peeked inside and smiled.

"Well I guess," he said.

"We better..." I nodded.

We walked into the empty foyer and up to the row of brightly lit vending machines. Sundar handed me a roll of packing tape and placed a flyer in the top right corner of one of the machines. As I pulled the tape across he put the next flyer in place beside it. We worked patiently, affixing our message of dissent.

The first month of the Social Justice Club was a triumph. A garage sale raised money for a local women's shelter. I consigned fair trade coffee, tea and chocolate from the OXFAM store downtown and we sold almost all of it one Friday afternoon.

We got permission to organize a political lecture series in the basement auditorium. Our first speaker was a hardcore kid affiliated with Ottawa's chapter of Food Not Bombs. He showed up with an envelope full of PETA propaganda and argued for veganism by describing the torturous lives and horrible deaths of livestock.

Attending the lecture allowed kids to miss class, so he had a large audience for his extreme opinions. In question period students tried to devise a way in which he would condone eating meat. "What if it was organic?" "What if you knew it was killed humanely?" To each of which he replied adamantly that it was still murder.

Sundar asked "What about leather?" The vegan didn't blink, despite his work boots. "I'll only wear *used* leather," he said, "but I don't feel *good* about it."

Our second guest was Bella Galhos, who had escaped her native East Timor. She spoke on the rape and genocide of her people at the hands of the Indonesians, who had occupied the nation since she was a child. After addressing crowds demonstrating outside the Indonesian embassy, her voice was strong. She detailed the forced injections of birth control and described the 1991 massacre in the city of Dili that she barely escaped.

After forty minutes of speaking and another twenty of answering questions, the square white light of an overhead projector appeared on the screen behind her, and we saw the shadow of a hand placing a transparency on its surface.

"This is the freedom song of my country. Please sing it with me." Then, accompanied only by the member of the East Timor Alert Network she had arrived with, she began to sing. The teenage audience tentatively voiced the words on the screen. "I'm still fighting," we sang lamely, but the passion of Galhos' rough edged voice impelled us to sing, to really sing.

Halfway through the song the bell rang; we had five minutes to get to our next class.

When we reached the end of the song she called "Again!" with tears streaming down her face, and we sang it again, even louder than before.

At our weekly meeting I suggested we do another OXFAM sale. Mr. Michel spoke up. "We can't do that. When I got clearance from the office it was one-time-only."

"Why?" I asked.

"Well," Mr. Michel said, "the school doesn't want to breach their contract with the company that runs the vending machines and the cafeteria."

"PepsiCo?" Sundar asked.

"No, a local distributor."

"But these are different..." I began. The chocolate bars were fair trade and cost five times more than those in the vending machine.

"So the school wants us to drink crappy coffee and eat bad candy AND NOTHING ELSE?" Alex said.

"They make a lot of money from it," Mr. Michel said.

The bell rang and as we gathered up our lunch bags and headed toward the door Alex muttered under his breath, "The system cannot be reformed."

A few days before this meeting Sundar had told me how he and his sister Sheela had spent their Friday afternoon. They got out the Yellow Pages and picked a Pizza Hut location at random. At the Fugazi show a flyer was circulated by the Canadian Friends of Burma. Singling out PepsiCo as the main corporate investor in Burma, it decried their support of oligarchy and urged a boycott of their galaxy of products and franchises, including Pizza Hut.

With the glee of someone who had never worked, Sheela called a franchise and pestered the voice on the other end with questions about Burma until she was transferred to the manager who gave her a number at headquarters before hanging up.

They climbed the corporate ladder via telephone. Each individual they spoke with professed to know nothing of their mothercorp's dealings with the small fascist-run Southeast Asian nation. The last person they talked to was a Regional Manager or perhaps even a Vice-President of Customer Relations (Canada) and when *they* professed to know nothing about Burma, Sheela finally became dramatic. "You don't KNOW anything about Burma? You don't THINK the house arrest of AUN SUN SUU KYI is a problem? SHE'S A NOBEL LAUREATE FOR PEACE!" She began laughing as soon as she slammed down the phone.

"Politically it was reactionary," Sundar told me. "We just angered and alienated several working people." He paused, thinking. "It still made for a fun Friday afternoon."

Two weeks later a coupon for a free pizza arrived in his mailbox. It said, "We're sorry your last Pizza Hut experience was unsatisfactory. Please try us again: On the house."

The day after my proposed OXFAM sale was shot down, Sundar and I had a strategy meeting in front of his locker at lunch. The physical fact of the vending machines was bad enough, we decided. They took up the places where the benches once sat. But on top of that, the products they sold propped up the Burmese oligarchy.

The local and global suddenly aligned; it was an activist miracle. It was then that we came up with this plan, the first stage of which was now complete.

The four vending machines were quilted in black and white flyers, held in place by packing tape. The flyers read, in large type, SUPPORT BURMA! BOYCOTT PEPSICO! The evidence was listed in smaller type below a graphic of the Pepsi logo with a cross through it.

"Yes!" we said, both hyper despite our lack of sleep.

We took one last look at our work. "That'll totally stay up."

By now more school buses were arriving and a few people were sleepily puzzling over the adapted vending machines.

We handed out the few left-over flyers before slipping away. I grabbed the giant cylinder and took it to Sundar's locker.

He unrolled it a bit, revealing the red and yellow on the inside. "I can't wait."

"Me neither."

I walked to my locker and slumped against it. The hallway slowly filled with snowboot-wearing teens. I pulled on my walkman and listened to Ian MacKaye shout: "You tell me that I make no difference / At least I'm fuckin' try-innnn' / What the fuck have *you* done?!"

A half hour before homeroom I was seized by a desire to return to the scene of the crime. The halls were now packed and I had to push against a tide of parkas and licensed sports-team jackets to make it back to the foyer.

I was expecting a smattering of students to have noticed the flyered vending machines and gathered around to read them and consider the evidence. Instead, what I saw made me instantly go mental.

Instead of finding a legion of newly politicized teenagers throwing the vending machines to the floor in a rage, I found the vice-principal, Mrs. Baird. Clad in a purple pantsuit, she was single-handedly dismantling our act of defiance, easily peeling off the dollar store packing tape that I'd put so much of my faith and allowance into.

"What are you doing?" I asked in total disbelief.

"These posters weren't stamped by the office." she said matter-of-factly. "They're not official."

"But—but!" How could I explain that the importance of this day trumped the petty rule that all posters put up in the school be approved by office staff.

"Also, they hide the products," she said, pulling off a section of flyers to reveal the rows of cookies and candy bars behind the machine's glass front.

"It's Free Burma Day," I said, and then corrected myself. "*International* Free Burma Day."

She looked me in the eye and said "I don't care."

My mouth went dry. How could I explain to her that for one day out of the year the struggle of the Burmese people must trump teenagers' right to access candy? As a sort of moment of silence on Remembrance Day kind of thing? I couldn't.

Soon, all our flyers were knotted in a giant ball of tape and thrown into a garbage can.

"Could we just put one up *next* to the machines?" I sputtered, willing to negotiate despite all my rage.

"No."

"But," I tried to reason "Aun Sun Suu Kyi—" I began.

"I don't care."

She didn't care about the imprisonment of the legally elected prime minister of Burma. She doesn't care, I thought. And then, if you don't care about Aun Sun Suu Kyi FUCK YOU.

When I was in high school I was often unable to control my emotions. For example, a year and a half before this incident I became extremely depressed when I heard Nirvana front-man Kurt Cobain had committed suicide. I couldn't stop myself from playing the three tapes I owned by the band over and over. At one point I placed one of my stereo speakers in my bedroom window so the whole world could hear my grief.

Angst was broadcast over the beautiful spring day, but because of my crappy stereo it was barely audible to the neighbours at work in their gardens.

The vice-principal threw another ball of tape and flyers into the steel garbage. "Get to home room," she said.

As she walked away the white hot rage coursing through my veins shaped itself into these words: "YOU'RE GOING DOWN BAIRD!" Which I then shouted at the top of my lungs.

She halted suddenly and turned to face me. My stomach sank. I thought of the consequences of what I said and felt nauseous. Nausea was soon replaced by the giddy feeling that I might just have ruined her morning.

"What did you say?"

"You heard me," I said, suddenly cocksure, despite my poor choice of words. At least the sentiment was correct. As she turned to face me I noticed that the kids passing through the foyer had stopped to watch.

"Come to my office. Now."

"No."

"That's it, you little..." She stopped short of saying what she wanted. "You're suspended for three days. Get your stuff and go. If you're still here in fifteen minutes the police will be called and you will be arrested for trespassing."

I had my riposte ready. "I don't care."

Behind my high school sat the municipal soccer fields and skating arena. Beyond was a warren of streets lined with grey and brown buildings, each bearing the name of their occupying company on the side. From these names alone it was impossible to infer what, if anything, these businesses made or did.

For the first two hours of my suspension I skulked around these streets, killing time. I finally settled down on one of the soccer pitches and ate my lunch, waiting. I watched the grey clouds and hoped the rain would hold off.

As 10:30 approached I moved closer to the fence, near the stile connecting the field to the school property. The fence was overgrown with vines but I could clearly see the track that ringed the football field.

From the school's doors a trickle and then a stream of students dressed in their grey gym t-shirts and sweatpants emerged, converging on the gravel track. Little pockets of dust erupted beneath their feet as they began to run, wheelbarrow walk, walk backwards or, for the most part, walk in a normal way around the track. It wasn't enough for 'The Grind' to be the school's annual fundraiser for the United Way; someone on student council thought that it would be even more fun if wacky walks were encouraged.

For what seemed like a very long time I watched small groups walking around the track, nervous until I finally saw a blur of yellow and red appear at the far end of the track and begin to move toward me at a steady pace.

Our secret weapon was in action. Seven people held it and walked together. The banner that I had carried to school unfurled to a length of ten feet. It bore a message of solidarity with the Burmese people and encouraged the boycott of Pepsi.

As they got closer I noticed the faces of the banner-holders were all appropriately solemn. It was a smattering of punks, goths and even Mikey, the cowboy. I watched them go by and waited for them to make another revolution before I pulled up the giant hood of my jacket and hoped no one would notice me casually walk out onto the track from the bushes and next to Sundar.

"It was fucking brilliant," he said of my outburst. He'd heard about it in homeroom. "In protest of our flyers getting pulled down the punks ripped down every flyer in the fucking school."

I laughed. "Isn't that reactionary?"

He smiled.

"I kind of screwed the club."

"We've been talking," he said. "We're going to disband the club and regroup out of school, because this is just fucking bullshit." I nodded.

After securing the lodging of the banner in Sundar's locker for the duration of my three day suspension I dropped back and thanked the banner carriers. I received high-fives and smiles.

I noticed Mr. Michel walking alone ten feet behind. I dropped back to talk to him.

"Did you hear?"

He nodded, unimpressed. "I don't know if that was the best way to handle the situation."

"No," I said, his disapproval making me feel ashamed for the first time.

"I don't see you," he said. "You're trespassing. I was told to call the police if I saw you."

I nodded and spun away, running to the property line.

II.

The foyer was transformed. There was a seething mass of pogoing and skanking bodies all the way back to the vending machines.

Standing on some risers assembled into a makeshift stage, with large speakers on either side of me, the sweaty palm of my right hand gripped a microphone.

The song ended. Behind me, Sundar strummed an open chord as the crowd filling the school's wide entryway howled in approval.

"Ready?" Kevin asked, standing to my left.

"Yeah," said Eric, anchored behind the drum kit.

I nodded.

In my hand was a flyer with the lyrics Bella Galhos had sung a few weeks before.

I told my mother I was going to the library for a few hours and pulled the hood of my parka against the wind. It was the hinge of the season. Two days before it had been warm enough to wear only a sweater, but today a dusting of snow covered the lawns and fallen leaves lined the curb.

When I reached the school I weaved through the lines of idling yellow buses. Sundar was waiting for me in the smoking section. He said hi and led me onto a bus. I followed him all the way to the back. When the bus finally started moving ten minutes later I caught a glimpse of Mrs. Baird standing by the doorway.

Sundar and I talked about punk rock and existentialism, neither of which we knew much about. He pulled a Tupperware container from his bag and offered me half a sandwich. I stared out the window as I ate, mouth full of peanut butter. The bus turned onto a long road. To the left was forest and to the right were farm fields.

The day after I first met him, Sundar had sold me a ticket to see his band play at an all-ages matinee. The appointed Sunday came and I took the bus downtown, walking from the Rideau Centre bus stop to the club nearby.

The Pit was a basement dive at the corner of Rideau and Dalhousie. It hosted all-ages matinees on the weekend. At least ten, sometimes as many as fifteen, bands played in a single afternoon. Teen music fans would emerge in the dwindling light of evening having dutifully watched all the local bands their five dollars would get them.

"Hi. We're Insanity Starts at Lake Erie, a shitty band from the suburbs," said the other guitarist of Sundar's band when they took the stage. The drummer nodded and the music began.

Their set was a whirl of feedback, pretty melodies and weird discordant shit that raked the hall but kept me rooted a few feet from the stage. They didn't have a singer or a bass player, just two guitars going in different directions, glued together by the drummer.

When the last song ended, the guitarist and drummer joined the meagre audience and watched Sundar as he crouched over his guitar and grabbed the butter knife sitting on his amp. He violently rammed it through the strings of his fake SG, pulling up and down the neck, producing sounds closer to those of the natural world than music. Roaring waterfalls, cicadas singing and the sound of the wind through the trees all came out of Sundar's black amp as he worked the knife. In a trance, he hit the guitar slightly for percussion and occasionally turned a knob on his distortion pedal.

Finally he stood up and turned off his amp. The sound still poured out of it for a moment before dying away. He stepped from the stage and walked across the floor and up the stairs.

The other guitarist hopped onto the stage and spoke into the microphone, "We need a..." when he realized the mic was off he paused for a second and then spoke un-amplified. "We need a singer and a bass player. So come talk to us."

Sundar returned and before taking apart his gear introduced me to Kevin, the other guitarist.

"I really like your band!"

He smiled. "Thanks, but I think we suck and need a bass player."

"No, the fact that you don't have one is cool."

"Well, thanks," Kevin said as he rolled up his patch chord.

The bus dropped us in a distant suburb far from the school. Sundar pointed out his house, a large one on the edge of a park. He led me past it to a small block of rowhouses and knocked on the door of the second last one.

Kevin opened the door. "Hey," he said to Sundar and then turned to me and mock-yelled *"You're going down Baird!"*

I laughed. "You heard about that at Confed?" My poorly-chosen words of rebellion had resounded through the halls of more than one school.

"Oh yeah, man."

Kevin handed us bowls of Kraft Dinner and we sat on the couch until Eric, the drummer, came in with a cymbal bag over his shoulder.

"You're going down Baird!" he said when he saw me sitting on the couch. He went to another high school too, not even the same one as Kevin. I groaned.

We left our empty bowls next to the kitchen sink and tromped downstairs to the basement where the amps and drum kit coexisted with a laundry line, washing machine and freezer.

Sundar wrote out the lyrics to the one song they had taught their last singer before he disappeared. It was called "Prole Feed." They played it through once and I figured out where the words went and then they played it again and I barked the lyrics into the microphone.

All week I had expected the International Free Burma Day protest to go smoothly and my audition for the Insanity Starts at Lake Erie to be gruelling. They were an actual *band*. Sundar had given me a practice tape recorded on a boombox and I rehearsed in my room with my headphones everyday. But when your pissed-off mother is downstairs, you have to scream quietly.

After a third run-through of "Prole Feed" Kevin said "Sounds good. You got any words for other songs?" I nodded and pulled out the notebook I'd been writing in for the last few months. Somehow my teenage writing, neither poetry nor prose, fit with the pretty chaos of their songs and we spent hours matching my words to their music. When the next-door neighbours started banging on the wall we turned the amps off and went upstairs.

The last light of day had disappeared. As we scheduled our next practice I realized this wasn't an audition; I was in the band. Kevin tried to explain the city bus routes back to my suburb until Eric offered to drive me home. I pulled on my boots and followed him over the icy sidewalk to his car. Once I was sitting shotgun he said "I've only got one tape in the car. One side is Miles Davis and the other is Minor Threat."

Earlier that day I directed the janitor to place the risers against the wall in between the boys' and girls' washrooms and supervised the AV club as they set up the small PA. All the while I thought it was amazing that my suspension hadn't voided my position as organizer of the second stage at the annual Band Warz competition.

"My fuckin' band is going to rule," Alex had promised me after I asked him to get a band together for the show. "The poseurs won't even be able to deal with it." The name of his band and its personnel were all kept secret until the day of.

Disgruntled, the band Alex had cobbled together from the dorks who hung out in front of my locker were actually pretty good. Alex was a surprisingly capable front man, with a sneer cemented to his face and a powerful delivery of "Banned from the Pubs" and a few other covers plus an original song or two. The crowd ate them up and Alex convinced me to give them a second set later in the evening. No one even noticed the songs were the same and skanked with the same fervour across the foyer floor.

And now I was on stage with The Insanity Starts at Lake Erie. "We sing this song in solidarity with Bella Galhos and the people of East Timor!" I yelled. "This song is called 'I'm Still Fighting'!" As teenage punk rock exploded all around me I began screaming.

> Many years passed by
> Many more to come
> Surrender? No never!
> Two hundred thousand
> Timorese have died yet
> Ramelau is as strong as ever
> Oh... I'm still fighting
> In my mountains
> In my jungle
> In the villages
> In the prisons
> I'm still fighting!
>
> In my mountains I feel free
> In my mountains I can smile
> In my mountains my song I can sing
> In my mountains I can dream
> In my mountains I can be me
> That's all I want
> I want to be free
> That's all I want
> I want to be me.

EPILOGUE:

Months later, on the coldest day of the year, I rode the bus downtown after school in the dark. I got off at the University of Ottawa and found my way to the offices of CHUO. I sat on a couch until the host appeared and led me into the studio.

It was a half hour interview show and the Social Justice Youth Collective (formerly known as Merivale High School's Social Justice Club) were the subject of the first fifteen minutes: our campaigns, what we accomplished, our beliefs, our ages (no one in the collective was over eighteen as a rule). The middle-aged radio host asked soft questions, impressed by our youth and our concern. At the end of the interview he pulled out the one tough question. "Do you really think you can change the world?"

I paused for a long time. *Did* I really think we could change the world? In the thick of scheming, planning and organizing it never came up.

"Even if," I began unsteadily, "we can't change the world, we can at least change ourselves."

The interview was over; I shook my questioner's hand as the new interviewee was ushered in. When I got home my mother told me she had listened to the interview with her mother and they both liked what I said about changing ourselves rather than the world. Then she served me spaghetti with meatless tomato sauce.

I don't know what, if anything, we changed. Fourteen years later Aun Sun Suu Kyi remains under house arrest. All I know is that when I was hiding in the bushes and saw the giant banner making its way slowly, solemnly, around the track I felt victorious. We had accomplished at least this, come together, worked hard and taken our beliefs seriously, even if we left no trace, no dent in the evil to which we were opposed.

All that's left is this story, and a mention on a long-dormant website:

The BurmaNet News: November 8, 1995
Issue #273: SPECIAL EDITION–OCT 27
CAMPAIGN RECAP

Meanwhile, the Social Justice Club at Merivale High School used our giant banner.

"Our protest was very... noticeable and it seems we have received quite a bit of attention for our cause, your cause. I support you completely, and it's honourable that there still ARE people who DO care... I am in the process of writing to Beaver foods who own several Pepsi machines in our school. I also intend to make complaints to many Pepsi-owned franchises."

(previously unpublished, 2007-09)

RECORD REVIEW
Sloan, *Twice Removed* (murderecords/DGC, 1994)

As they approach the ninth or tenth grade white high school students are drawn magnetically to the pole of pop culture that is The Beatles. One day they find themselves in the basement looking through their parents' record collection lodged in a particleboard bookshelf. There they inevitably find *Red* and *Blue* by The Beatles and become suddenly obsessed; buying posters, t-shirts, and countless books of Fab Four ephemera and being so smug that their favourite band is quantifiably THE best pop band ever, and aren't the lyrics just so meaningful and let's talk about it all the time.

Beatlemania hit my shitty friends in my shitty suburb thirty years late and I didn't buy into it. Yeah, the songs were catchy and insanely orchestrated, but so what?

I grumbled when my friends Beatle'd out, but what did I have? I didn't have shit—a Sex Pistols tape from the Music Mart discount bin was the only weapon in my arsenal and I didn't even know what it meant. "God Save the Queen"? Were they joking? Like the *Queen*? That woman that does nothing and who no one cares about is the target of your vitriol? Really?

The day *Twice Removed* came out I walked to the mall, my walkman hungry for a new tape. They were just a one hit wonder from Halifax in the age of grunge long since past, but the Ottawa *Citizen* Entertainment section advised me this new record was pure sweet pop and an imperishable classic.

It was a step in the wrong direction. I wanted to be punk but I didn't know how and needed to listen to something in the meantime. Plus, I couldn't get the single that played all the time on Much Music out of my head. It had this plaintive guitar line that was so melancholy and was such a perfect fit for mid-August when I hated my friends and school loomed on the horizon like an iceberg to my Titanic summer self.

Walking home through the rowhouses, the music washed over me. All these sad pop songs about funerals and brothers and snowsuits and pen-pals. It was a perfect slice of Canadiana moulded into pop and caught in the amber of magnetic tape.

(A few months later at their show I nervously asked the drummer if I could interview him for the crappy zine I was making. I didn't even have a tape recorder, just tried to write down the things he said on some bar napkins. He was nice and when he discovered I'd never heard The Descendents he strongly recommended I find a copy of *Milo Goes to College*. I did.)

(Ghost Pine #9: Bees, 2005)

7

NO TIME

TWO HOURS LATE, BRENDAN PULLED UP IN FRONT OF MY apartment in his dad's grey station wagon. He hopped out of the driver's side door and helped me wedge my bag into the back.

"Sorry it's so crowded, maaan." The trunk was packed with a drum kit, bags of cables, his eight-track mixer and glittering loose CDs. Brendan was going to spend the summer in Maine making a record in a barn. But first he was taking me to his hometown of Williamsburg, Virginia.

His baseball cap read Atlantic City and that seemed like an appropriate approximation of what went on in his head. Were his skull to be cracked open it would reveal the casino of his mind—thousands of flashing lights and slot machines into which he inserted the coins of artistic ideas. Whether for a movie, a comic strip, or a song, they would almost always pay out.

"Maaan," he said in his laziest southern accent, "we're going to my homeland! The motherfuckin' U.S. of A!" He punched the steering wheel as the car rolled down avenue Du Parc and then hunched over, deep in concentration.

"Is driving hard?" I asked him, having never been behind the wheel of a car.

"Naah, it's easy." He paused before exclaiming "Oh shit! Let me tell you about this one time, down in Virginia. By where I grew up there are all these really tight roads, where you gotta, like, always have your hands on the wheel or else you're going to end up in the ditch. So one day I was driving around there. Had my shirt off, windows down, feelin' good, blasting some tunes on the radio, when I see this dead squirrel in the road. The thing was completely flattened, so I didn't bother swerving. Even if I had there was nowhere to go but into the oncoming traffic, right? So I drive over the squirrel. Whatever right? But then I'm driving and I feel something on my left hand and I look down... It's the fucking squirrel! When I went over it, it flew up and onto my hand, and I was driving these tight roads so it was, like, twenty minutes before I could get this corpse off my hand."

Brendan and I met on Valentine's day. I had seen him around before then, at shows or tiny art openings at the university. He wore a blue parka everywhere he went. It was covered in splatters of red paint and an assortment of treasures he pulled from alley floors; random pieces of fabric and part of a lambskin rug were safety-pinned to his coat. Shoelaces and bracelets were tied to his wrists.

We met at a puppet show in an old stone theatre and when we discovered that we lived near each other we decided to walk home together, up Du Parc. He told me he had decided to move to Montreal after one spring break when, on a whim, he and two friends drove thirty-six hours through a blizzard to reach the city. Once they arrived, they only had enough time to have a cup of coffee before turning back. "It wasn't even a cool café, just one of those crappy places on the Main. But for some reason I still thought 'I like this town,'" he laughed.

In the months that followed I ran into him at the café where I went every day to read before crossing the street to write in my office—a library built in the shell of an old church. One day he sat down at my table in the crowded café. "Look, I know you're reading but there's nowhere else to sit." I told him I would happily converse with him and he looked at me enraged.

"No! You are a writer!" he said gravely. "It is of the utmost importance that you read!" He grabbed the book I had been reading compulsively and for half an hour read me tales of elves and dwarves in an enchanting voice. The voice was sort of similar to the narrator from the old *Dungeons and Dragons* Saturday morning cartoon, but a pinch more scholarly, and with a bit of an English accent thrown in for good measure. I was just halfway through the book at that point and as I read the remaining pages, it was with Brendan's immaculate narration in my head.

As the spring warmed up we eschewed the café, buying take-out tuna sandwiches and sitting in an abandoned boxcar up by the train tracks. On one April day when winter refused to give up the ghost and blew hard through the boxcar, we slipped through a hole in the fence that surrounded the trainyard. We bought a bottle of wine, went into an *apportez votre vin* Indian restaurant and ordered some sweets.

We sat at the front of the restaurant. Outside the skies were dull and leaden and had been that way for as long as I could remember.

"I'm sick of this," I said, "working at the bakery, love affairs that go nowhere and grey skies forever."

Brendan looked at me, dead serious, and said "We can go anywhere."

So while he drew a picture on his placemat of a scene from a jungle he wanted to visit, I drew a map of North America on mine and put stars on the cities I wanted to go to.

Two months later, I had quit my job, given up my huge bedroom and was en route to the first destination of my placemat map. We were rapidly leaving behind the border crossing where the tightly arranged farmhouses of southern Quebec gave way to the wide rolling pastures of Vermont. Visiting the rest of the placemat stars would take three months in total.

As the sun fell into the horizon, Brendan explained his latest project to me. "I'm writing eight hundred songs. Each one of them is inspired by a piece of trash, or some artifact I found on the streets of Mile End. I just stare at the thing for a while..." he stopped talking for a second.

"Well, to fully explain it to you I've got to tell you about this realm I go into sometimes." I raised my eyebrows. "It's where I go when I'm working on art. When I'm writing or recording a song, or working on a comic I enter the world of No Time, where time doesn't matter, in fact it doesn't even exist."

I nodded empathetically. "Oh you just think I'm crazy." He waved his hand.

"No, no. I know about No Time. When I go to the library to write every afternoon I take off my watch and put it in my pocket."

"Yeah." A smile broke across his face and he resumed explaining the eight hundred songs. "So I'll concentrate on the thing and then set up my room with all the mics and record all the different tracks. Then I mix them on my computer and put them on the Internet. Okay, okay, I know it's cheesy, but there are pictures of the objects that inspired the songs on my"—he made the quotation marks symbol with his right hand—"webpage," he laughed, "and when you click on the picture it plays the song."

"So how many songs are left?"

"About seven hundred and forty, but I'll write them in no time."

On the right side of the highway a lake appeared. "Let's take a break," he said, pulling the station wagon onto the shoulder. We walked through the tall grasses that ringed the lake until we each found sticks and spontaneously began sword-fighting.

Brendan's sword was two-pronged and he named it Grackle. His voice returned to the one that he had used to narrate a chapter of *The Lord of the Rings* months ago. Except now it was tinged with realm-conquering evil. "Many shall fall before my Grackle, and I shall rule this universe!"

He lunged at me and hit me hard on my right hand, suddenly reverting to his normal voice. "DUDE, dude! I'm sorry!"

I rubbed my sore paw. "It's okay," I said.

It was.

(Ghost Pine #8: Wolf, 2004)

OFFICES

WHEN LIFE, THAT WIDE ARRAY OF STUFF THAT STEALS AWAY TIME, gets in the way of my writing, I often moan that the root problem is not that I have five papers due on the same day or that I have to sweat to make rent. No, instead I moan about the fact that I don't have an office.

This craving for a secret piece of real estate to put my desk and lamp was kick-started one day when I was leafing through a glossy rock magazine and came across a picture of dark songster Nick Cave sitting at a grand piano. The byline to the photo, which was not much larger than a postage stamp, explained that this was the interior of Cave's office where he wrote songs every day from nine to five. While I knew I would never have enough money for a grand piano, I imagined me and my desk there in the place of Cave and his instrument. It felt good.

That said, in the last decade of writing and publishing *Ghost Pine* there have been a total of three instances where I was offered office space, and I failed to use it every time.

The first offer came from a kindly café employee who gave me free refills regularly for two months before telling me that I could bring in my own CDs to play on the stereo if it would help me with my writing. It wasn't exactly office space, but this barista was kind to me in my time of need. I was working the morning shift at the doughnut shop and in the afternoons I retired to the café to examine the wreckage of my life via scrawling into a notebook. This café guy was a ray of light in my darkest day so, of course, I immediately stopped going to the café. After years of wanting to attain 'regular' status somewhere I was forced to admit that I preferred a sort of friendly anonymity.

The next offer came from Mackenzie. When he first moved to Montreal he had a long string of house-sits and then moved into an apartment above the old Aux Vivres on St. Dominique that had been evicted to make way for the landlord's condo dreams. Mackenzie snuck in and stayed for months, from fall into winter, thanks in no small part to the electric baseboard heaters. He painted the walls pink and added giant stencils of the words HOME SWEET HOME across them.

One night I went to see him, fresh from visiting my mom's house. We cooked up the barley soup she'd given me on the hot plate, dipping pieces of her banana bread in it, open Ephemeres sitting beside us on the floor.

"You know, I have an extra room here," he said. "If you want to use it as an office go right ahead."

Awesome. Of course there was the small problem of my living on the other side of town, down in the Pointe. By the time I went over to do some writing a few weeks later Mackenzie's band, The Let Lowns, were practicing in my office. Then the landlord came by with some workers. It was the final eviction. I helped the band carry their amps down the stairs and sat them in a snowbank. Three years later Mackenzie's old squat has yet to be demolished. It just sits there, all boarded up and covered in posters.

The most recent friends whose goodwill I've thwarted are Sarah and Sonia, who invited me to do a residency at the Anchor Archive in 2006. They even went as far as cleaning out the back shed and built a bunk in it (and the last line in my most recent zine was "I've yet to live in a shed." I'm prophetic!). Best of all, one half of the loft bed was a leaf that could be pulled out to transform the bed into a desk. Amazing!

Did I ever write in the shed? Of course not. Spike (who was historian-in-residence) and I slept in it for the duration of our residency but every morning we trudged through the rain to the other archive in town, the big provincial one, where Spike did research and I got a ton of writing done. At the end of the day we came back to the shed that housed us and made our amazing 'working holiday' possible. Sitting in the backyard drinking Propeller I.P.A. I was always happy to know that my work was sequestered across town and I'd get back to it the next day.

What does all this tell you? Well, number one, I'm an asshole who somehow has great friends, and number two, never

listen to me if I whine about not having enough space to work in. All I've ever needed is a flat surface, a notebook and a pen.
(Anchor Archive Regional Zine Project Newsletter #4, 2006)

NEPEAN

"so..."

"Yeah," Chris said.

It was awkward. We were both back in the suburbs for Christmas and after a while without seeing each other we had both arrived at Denny's for our midnight coffee wearing nearly identical blue plaid shirts. Our black jeans, toques and glasses were pretty similar too.

After a few moments of silence following our hug Chris said "It's like when people find out they were separated at birth from a twin and then when they meet they're wearing the exact same clothes."

From our booth, I could see that the Merivale Road Denny's had not changed. The booth's naugahyde lining showed no wear, the tables were un-chipped and the hood above the fry station gleamed as if it had just been installed. The nights Chris and I had spent here had not left a single mark. The only change of any significance were the higher prices on the menu.

This brightly lit diner was never our favourite. A few strip malls further down Merivale Road sat Briskets. My parents often asked me how a restaurant named after a cut of beef could be the hangout of every vegetarian punk in a three mile radius. The answer, as always, is one part free coffee refills and one part cheap fries. Also, the interior was covered in mahogany, or at least painted brown, and the lighting was dim. On a street of fast food franchises the dark smoky interior came off as infinitely more aged and bohemian than, say, the Zellers cafeteria across the street.

Chris had worked there as a dishwasher as had Graeme before him. I spent hours, freshly graduated from high school and unemployed, drinking refills and waiting for my two friends to finish their shifts so I could drink more coffee with them. I wasted a whole winter full of days that way.

Chris, Graeme and I were writers. We piled the books we had read on the table between us and excitedly declared the brilliance of each one. We also discussed our grandiose plans for our new zines and the photocopying techniques we would use to make them. It went on like this for hours.

One day, when the snow was beginning to melt, I decided that my spring-board to fame and fortune would be winning the five hundred dollar grand prize of the Nepean Short Story Contest. It was advertised on the community bulletin board at the strip mall library where I hid when I told my mother I was looking for work.

I cleaned up one of the stories written for my zine and saved the fifty cents on the stamp by walking it over to city hall. I paid the five dollar entry fee with a fistful of change, much to the chagrin of the secretary in charge of submissions.

A few months later I received a letter telling me I had won a prize in the contest, but would have to attend the award ceremony to discover how I'd placed. So one May evening, as the birds sang well into prime time, my mother climbed into her favourite purple frock and my father into one of his suits. They drove me to city hall where we were directed to the council chambers.

I was disappointed when I was awarded only runner up. Instead of recognition and cash I walked away with a brass bookmark bearing the library's motto, "Libraries are the Link!" And yet the look of pride on my mother's face was worth it. Later she consoled me by saying that all the other winners were at least fifteen years older than me.

At the reception afterwards a slightly flustered librarian from the panel of judges approached me and apologized in a British accent. "I'm sorry I couldn't give you a better placing, I really did love your story. Please do keep writing."

Four months later, in a tiny room in the main branch of the Nepean library, my parents again climbed into their dress and jacket to hear me read, along with the other victors. I went first and read far too fast, stumbling through and feeling my face turn a shade of red. Listening to the other award winners read I finally conceded that their stories were better than mine. I had a long way to go. Chris and Graeme were in the small audience, and despite my stilted reading cheered loudly when I finished. We had already made plans to go the sports bar across the parking lot when the readings were over.

(Ghost Pine #11: Crows, 2007)

8

LUCKY RON AT CHATEAU LAFAYETTE

"IT'S GOOD YOU GOT HERE EARLY," MY BROTHER SAID, NOTICING the fat asses on stools and the thick elbows on every available inch of table in the bar. In the twenty minutes I'd been waiting for him, men had streamed into the bar, alone or with friends and gladly boarded the seats of their afternoon drunk.

"Oh god, The Laf, eh?" he said returning to the table, bottle in hand. Although this was my brother's regular thing, he hadn't seen Lucky Ron play since the show moved over here.

In the last five years the Byward Market had become fully saturated by 'authentic Irish pubs,' their decor and dormroom-rehearsing Celtic musicians attempted to evoke a false ancient Erin out of the fogs of Hibernian history.

The Laf was different. It was the only place in an old neighbourhood with a connection to yesteryear. Established these one hundred and fifty years it was nearly going under because its history wasn't kitsch. Its lineage was fluorescent lit and ugly; it was in the dust bunnies and bottle caps collecting beside the turquoise baseboard.

Still, Chateau Lafayette had seen all the shit. Saw funeral processions of malaria deaths and then Spanish influenza deaths and then murder and then old age. Saw bloody riots in the streets, the protestant Micks pounding Hab and Paddy papists and the Paddies pounding the Peasoupers and then and then. Everyone just pounding the shit out of everyone like sometimes you'll see when the bars let out, or imagine when you see blood on the pavement the next day.

The Laf saw the hundreds who filed into town from Valley farmsteads to witness the hanging of Patrick Whelan. Then saw the apocalyptic blizzard that hit the very next day, stranding for weeks those bloodthirsty assholes who came to see the Fenian killed.

Saw the lumberjacks riding corduroy roads Bytownwards from Algonquin after the May melt. Their purses full and their pricks hard after a winter of sodomy and hard work and baked beans; near jumping out of their skins for woman, bath and bottle.

Saw me come in this afternoon and sit and wait for my brother and saw me greet him twenty minutes later when he came in the door.

Somewhere in the fluid time of beer and conversation a man wearing a cowboy hat appeared. All eyes were glued to him as he crossed the jammed bar floor and mounted the stage in the corner. He grabbed the acoustic guitar, turned on the loud speaker and shouted "Now I taught that weeping willow how to cry cry cry" and his voice did not have a rest until a dozen songs were sung.

Banter was limited to the topics of the songs. These were "Train songs!" "Prison songs!" or "Hurtin' songs!" and his country songbook was some kind of weird atlas charting the uncertain geography of manhood. The fingers of his left hand danced across the fret-board and we cried approval over the boom of his voice.

It was the twenty-first year of Lucky Ron's Sunday matinee. The first set was at four p.m.—afternoon in the summer and twilight by November. After intermission the second set began at that beery hour when you knew you should probably be getting home but the crowded path to the door and the cold wind scraping the streets outside made you think better of it.

My brother was a loyal fan who had seen the show thirty times or more in the last five years. He sang when he knew the words, louder when it was a Stompin' Tom number, and when it was June Carter's "Ring of Fire" his voice reached a near-laryngitis-inducing howl. He pounded an empty quart bottle in time until it broke into three pieces on the table. Watching my skinny brother, dressed in a button-down shirt tucked into his jeans, smash a beer bottle had me laughing hysterically.

As I cracked up, late-departing Canada geese flew V-style far over the roof of the bar. They felt the post-Hallowe'en cold in their bones, just like our drunk selves, and were struggling ever further south just as they had for all time.

(Ghost Pine #11: Crows, 2007)

RIDING THE 95

THE BEST PART OF RIDING THE 95 IS WHEN IT EMERGES FROM THE cement channel of the bus-only Transitway and pulls up past Merkeley Bricks, where the back façade of the wall is made up of every different brick design and colour they carry.

Next to that, separated by a small chain link fence, is the mountain of snow: the place where the dump trucks full of snow unload. By the end of winter it's humongous and doesn't fully melt until September.

Following that is the old, long-grown-over train tracks and bridges now populated by bad tagger crews, rather than the coal engines of old.

Far off to the right is the "City Centre" office and ware-houses and the line of houses fading away, marking the border of Mechanicsville.

To the left are more rusted track and rotten ties and bridges that kids fish or dive off of into the dead river.

It's all grassland now, a cordoned-off road and endless tangles of paved bike path hidden by hills and tress that no one planted.

Further to the left is the Hull skyline of government buildings and the paper mill—across the river and in an altogether different province. And language.

And straight in front Ottawa rises up. Up on a hill with

blocky buildings. From here I can see all of it. From outside.

Then a twist and a turn and we quickly pass by the campgrounds sitting strong under the hill of Ottawa. Just outside the gates.

Then another turn up a treed hill and I pass through the invisible city gates. Suddenly I'm on the other side of the wall and in the grids and canyons so alien as I made my way past all the crazy grasslands.

The first thing greeting me is the park across the street from the tech high school. Where all the kids who cut their teeth down by the abandoned tracks and cement bridges come to do aerosol work. Too bad most of the kids suck. The current graf champ is the huge African face sprayed to look like it's pressed up to glass. It has the whole town talking. I hope the taggers give it props and don't spray over it tonight or next week.

As the geography shifts once in the city, I shift too. Rather than being a nameless suburban teen that lives in a place where nothing happens but inertia I feel my possibilities become endless.

In the city I can have soup and roast kosher marshmallows on the candles at Lesley's, skate for pie with the Apache Devils gang, see a punk show, hang out with Matt and Kiana at the park, see Mike F. the rock star at his job at the library and sit on a sunny stoop. All in under twelve hours.

(Otaku #3, 1997)

TEAM OF SERVICE REPRESENTATIVES

AT 6:20 A.M. ON ANY GIVEN WEEK DAY OTTAWA'S STREETS ARE quiet and nearly empty. The only people scurrying to and fro wear burgundy pants and bags under their eyes.

Today I was wearing those burgundy pants, part of the mass-issued uniform of the biggest doughnut shop chain in

Canada, my employer for the past month. I walked inside the store; only ten to seven and the line was already spilling out onto the street.

I stared at the customers with contempt, heading to the back room for a fresh hair net, the beginning of a shitty day like any other.

Or so I thought. "Hey," Sundar waved to me nonchalantly from behind the cash, a fresh new burgundy uniform hanging off his willowy frame, "I took your advice."

I remembered seeing him at some party the week before, but forgot the obviously brilliant advice I'd imparted to him. "What did I tell you?"

"That this job sucks, but you make twice as much as welfare." He played awkwardly with his name tag. It read, "Hi, my name is Warren, I'm in training." The only training name tag in the store.

"Warren, I'd like a large double double," barked an impatient woman in line.

I retired to the back room, clipped on my tie, stole a fresh sour cream doughnut from the rack, and pondered the latest addition to our team of service representatives.

Sundar and I were in an art punk band together in high school, and even then he was sticking rulers and butter knives through the strings of his guitar. These days he was following his dream of becoming an avant-garde musician, occasionally flying to New York City to play in an orchestra comprised of a hundred guitarists.

Here at home he played many shows where he would simply slip a cassette of himself playing in a ghetto blaster, press Play and then sit doing nothing while everyone looked at each other anxiously. Here I was, working with a genius, each at our own cash register asking "Small, medium, large, or extra large?" five hundred times a day.

When I got called in for my interview at the doughnut shop I was filled with thoughts of small town doughnut joints, a gathering place for the community, quietly possessing a sense of despair coupled with dignity, the tables populated with laid-off factory workers or miners. The pace would be so laid back I would have long, noncommittal political debates and benign conversations about the weather with customers.

No such luck. My particular doughnut shop was located beneath the glass towers of the financial district. While I sold coffee for minimum wage, men in suits were lighting cigars with my friends' savings, sitting around a gleaming oak conference table on the fortieth floor of nearby buildings, devising new tactics to lure us further into debt.

Every city has these same canyons of glass. By day the streets overflow with hurried pedestrians, bike messengers and the cars that open their doors on them. By night the only sound is the occasional spinning of skateboard wheels. Kids fly off marble stairwells or run from grey-haired security guards. Homeless men work methodically through the garbage cans, looking for pop cans and other treasures. The office building lights turn black one by one as cleaning staff work their way through disposing of mountains of shredded paper.

I can barely explain the slow pour of a graveyard shift. Customers came at three hour intervals, and I sat reading, desperately trying to fill out the hollow hours. Staring out the window I watched patterns of white and black forming and dissolving as snow fell over the city. I served cabbies with skin the colour of two hour old coffee, and cops with skin like sugar-covered raspberry doughnuts. Regardless of creed or class, we all use coffee to beat up the night.

Back on the day shift a security camera had been installed. I began to wonder where my image was being broadcast. Was it just on the closed circuit TV in the manager's office? Could the signal be sent to the owner's house? Head office? Was my image being digitized and my actions shown on some obscure webpage watched by the world's bored and idle? Was I unwittingly being turned into a series of ones and zeros, flickering on and off?

My paranoia grew daily, and Sundar became my sounding board. "Sundar," I said, as we rapidly tried to clean in a rare period of calm. "Do you think we can chart society's decline through architecture?" I stuck a metal pipe cleaner known as 'the snake' up a coffee maker and pushed and pulled it vigourously.

"First the tallest buildings were churches, totally repressive but at least based on some ideal of hope. Next came the smoke-stacks of the industrial revolution, a symbol of mindless work. And now the tallest buildings belong to the debt mongers: the fucking bank towers."

He stared blankly, "You're wrong. The tallest structures these days are TV broadcast towers."

I crossed the Laurier bridge twice daily. Once to work and once to freedom. Crossing in the morning I noted the colour of the sky and the water level of the canal. Every day the clock of the Peace Tower informed me how late I was for work. Sometimes the world was swallowed by a thick veil of spring fog, and this morning it completely erased the Parliament buildings from the skyline. Staring into nothing, I scrawled in my notebook, "Let's bring down the government one foggy six a.m. at a time, let's erase the government from our own foggy minds."

(Ghost Pine #6, 2001)

THE ANNUAL GREAT GLEBE GARAGE SALE REPORT, 1998

THE BUS DRIVER SUMMED IT UP. "I HOPE YOU AREN'T ALL GOING TO the Great Glebe Garage Sale, it's been cancelled, the weather's too good! Ha." Everyone else laughed too, nervously hoping they weren't missing out on the find of their life as the bus crawled through Bank Street traffic.

Another year and it was still interesting to see the streets of the Glebe overrun by bargain hunters of all stripes. Unfor-tunately I made the obvious mistake of wearing clean clothes and shoes without holes. I should have found some way to look dirtier. No one believed me when I told them I only had five measly bucks to my name. It was true though, my boss is so slow on pay the glaciers will melt and flood this city before I get paid for the tours I did.

Sympathy was thin. One grey-haired yuppie tried to sell me a skateboard with a "Kids" sticker on it for twenty bucks! I almost spit in his face even though I'm sure I'll spend at least twice that on trucks when I inherit Damien's old deck. But still, it's the principle of the thing.

Admittedly the Glebe is probably the worst neighbourhood in the world to hold a garage sale, considering it's populated by yuppies, snobby rich kids, ambassadors and aging hipsters —all the people that don't understand the delicate symbiotic relationship between the garage saler and the bargain fiend. We take their old junk off their hands and they give us cheap prices. No questions need be asked, it's a precious slow dance and everyone wins. Not so in the Glebe.

I thought I'd made *the* find when I unearthed some old Cramps and Exploited LPs from one of the few piles of records in the hood. But when I asked the price they were fifteen each since they were "collector's items." Not only was I too broke to pick 'em up, I couldn't buy them out of plain principle. The fun of getting punk stuff is that no one else knows what it is. No one knows that it has a secret value, not monetary but the value of knowing that punk records are novels written out across your heart while all the other records in the pile are just bad one-liners. Buying an old Fugazi record or *Cometbus* zine off someone's well-tended lawn is more fun than getting them through the regular channels.

Worst of all were the piles of junk left over from kids who left home for university. Since I'm the age where I should be following that path I had to watch all the bad trends of my youth flash before my eyes.

Still, despite all the bad it's always nice to see people out in the sun trying to haggle over the price of used shower curtains. Garage sales are so interesting because they make you redefine what's valuable and you get to see what others value most too. And as a kid who still hasn't learned how to use computers it was rewarding to see once-valuable PCs piled next to the *Peanuts* pocket books and old jazz 78s. The new technology has the same value as the old: I could buy a math program or an abacus for the same price: one dollar, no refunds.

(Otaku #4, 1999)

O-TOWN PRAYER

WHAT DO I DO AFTER A WEEK LONG TRIP? HEAD DOWNTOWN alone, hopeful I'll run into my lover, the main character in all my stories. Right into the storm and stress of the city, black clouds forming high above the north of Laurier skyscrapers. The suits are pulling at their ties nervously.

I look for her in one of those secret Bank St. buildings, but I just get caught in the elevator for the second time this week. I wonder if she'll swoop in and save me but I'm not surprised when she's a no-show and I'm left to escape on my own.

She's been dodging me lately. Avoiding meeting me on the street and leaving parties before I get there. She thinks I'm hot stuff, just like the Rideau Centre Luv Doctor machine but she worries about my cheating heart. She worries when I'm away that I'm falling for someone else, somewhere else.

I can't find her so I go about my post-trip decompression alone. Going to the office for the cheque I've been waiting for. All the doors are locked of course. No signs of life.

Back on the street, what do I do after a week of being constrained in a crowded, sticky and scorching music hall? Might as well get on the packed rush hour Bank Street bus. What do I do after a week of dodging romance? Fall in love with the girl on the street as I pass. My life's stupid symmetry unravels.

Similarities end when I get stuck in a bus shelter waiting for the storm to break and then turn to see the sun still shining the next block over. So after a week of hanging out with kids because of our shared rebellion I make friends in the bus-shelter. A support group for victims of typical Ottawa Valley weather. Delicately swapping gossip on the tornado looming large. One lady shakes her fist: "Damn you El Niño!" and our solidarity is sealed with laughter.

What do I do after a weekend of too many guitars and too many tables of records? I skip down to the record shop, pick up the classic punk LP Andy ordered in for me. The one I was ashamed to admit was missing from my milk crate. My honey is still M.I.A. so I head down the block. What do I do after a week of unwarranted insomnia and uninterrupted fourteen-hour drives? Well, nothing could be better than an injection of caffeine. Might as well spend my last dollar at the diner, you know, the one with the worst cup of coffee in town and the slowest refills thrown in for free. Still, this place keeps pulling me back. I'm hooked on its post 2 a.m. scene. Watching the chaos of a diner filled to the brim with every punk, alky, drunk, yuppie, club kid and down and out in the whole city milling about. Everyone is too drunk to exert the pretension that seems to come so natural at every other dive in town.

Plus my honey might come by and see me writing my dumb stories in the window. Too bad she never shows, or maybe she already did. I had my back to the window. Window seats are only for the lonely.

Since she doesn't show I head up Elgin; these streets have a perfect way of tying things together while still leaving plenty of contradictions out in the open. Like, if Bank Street is the gay village how come only hicks hang around that block? If Elgin is so perfect and prosperous how come it has the highest density of panhandlers per block in the whole city?

Speaking of Elgin street panners, I give shout outs to the "care to spare some change to support lesbian street trash" girl. Shit yeah! That line has worked on me more than once.

Night is falling and I've got one last place to maybe run into my lover. I pull into the library, say hello to the rock star working the desk and proceed to rot until eight o'clock closing. I pick up a book in the kids' racks about a boy who rides a motorbike since it's the mechanical embodiment of rock 'n' roll. It got me to thinking about what punk rock would be if it were a machine. My guess is it would be a broken-down tour van, that, like punk itself, never seems to get anywhere. Either that or a photocopier that runs on the 'honour system.'

Back to the street I'm still anxious and knotty stomach-ed about that girl and my lack of her. But walking to the bus stop I catch a glimpse of her running down another side street, escaping me all over again. There she goes; between reading between the lines in the cement library and getting harangued by the assholes of Rideau Street. Getting splashed by the puddles on the snaky broke-tooth smile of St. Laurent to the last chance salvation of the big blue neon cross that stamps the sky across the river.

As the sun sets there she is, illuminated in her most flattering light. There she is, the heroine of all my stories, my sweet lover, smiling shyly: this city of O-Town. Across the trainbridge, across my heart. And all she holds.

(Otaku #4, 1999)

CANADIAN THANKSGIVING

"YOU DIDN'T CALL ME THERE, A FEW MONTHS BACK," SAID MATTY. I looked at the two hundred and fifty pounds of muscle that comprised my Lebanese cousin.

"Hm, how's that?" I asked. I was already feeling the effects of the three pre-dinner beers I pilfered from my uncle Ian's fridge.

"I need the description of two mugging motherfuckers," he said.

"Ah," I nodded.

It happened one night last summer as I strolled through the abandoned financial district after work, making my way to the bus stop. Near Bank Street, two guys were walking toward me down the sidewalk. I paid them no mind; even from a distance I could tell they were members of that most unfortunate caste, the Ottawa Valley crackhead.

When they grabbed me I thought it was an old fashioned fag bashing. To this day, Ottawa offers the full spectrum of hate crime, from continual shouts out of passing cars that assail anyone not clad head-to-toe in Nike apparel, right up to men being thrown off cliffs because of who they choose to fuck.

"What do you want?" I screamed, covering my head as they dragged me into a vacant parking lot. For the benefit of the legions of tourists who visit the Ottawa downtown core every year, this particular parking lot was surrounded by waist high shrubs, part of the city's latest beautification project.

The smaller of the two men had a long, rat-like face. He wore a Beatles t-shirt with the arms cut off. "How much money you got in your bank account?" he hissed.

"Maybe seventy bucks?" I was generous with my estimate.

Rat-face's companion was thicker and taller. He, no doubt, was the muscle of the operation; he wore a shirt barely covering the circumference of his belly. He motioned for me to hand him my wallet, and he rifled through my riches, which comprised a five dollar bill, a loonie, and OC Transpo bus tickets for my ride home. The muscle pushed me to the ground, tripping my feet from under me. He held a sharp rock tight to my throat and barked, "What's your fuckin' PIN number?"

As I told them, I remembered that I created my bank card's PIN in homage of a Shotmaker song, itself a series of numbers. I thought about this, quite possibly the nerdiest act I'd ever committed, as a strange man held me down with a rock to my throat. For a second I could almost watch myself, years ago, typing it in on the keypad for the first time.

The rat-faced man made a beeline for the ATM in the marble-floored lobby of an office tower across the street. The muscle watched me anxiously, making sure I didn't escape pending the PIN's authenticity. I slowly stood up and looked him in the eye.

Later, I would examine mug shot after mug shot of his ilk. A slow-motion slide show, the images changing with the click of the mouse. "I'm just going down the hall. You call me if you see the perps," the plainclothes constable said, after showing me to a computer in the depths of the police headquarters. "This database has mugs of Caucasian men, aged twenty through forty-five, all taken in the last five years."

And thus unrolled hundreds of faces. The pictures changed, but the characteristics rarely did. They all had shaggy hair, and more than a few of them were bleeding from the head. Inset next to some of the faces were digital photos of blue-green tattoos of snakes, 'Mom,' and maple leafs. Everyone had facial hair, most of the moustache variety so unpopular in recent years.

Who are these men? These are party boys from up the Valley. They grew up in Maniwaki, Pembroke, Renfrew, and came to the city in search of kicks. Their demand for higher peaks of hedonism than the banal teenage fun of shotgunning cans of Molson Ex and sniffing airplane glue had lured them down-valley to freebasing cocaine in the big smoke.

Or perhaps these men fled their home towns when someone close to them broke their heart (or threatened to actually *have* the baby). As refugees from everything they had ever known, they found only one solace, one light at the end of the tunnel: the light at the end of a crack pipe. The haze fogging their heads helped them forget the harsh realities that came with being a high-school dropout, broke, and living in a scabies-infested rooming house behind the bus station in a city obsessed with money and education.

Clicking from one mug to the next, I remember briefly experiencing this brand of men before. We crossed paths at the welfare office, under the Queensway that cuts the city in two. As I nervously bit my nails before my first appointment with a case worker, I noticed all the other men in the waiting room were clad in skin-tight acid wash jeans and shod in untied salt-stained work boots. They were continuously making demands of the well-groomed gay receptionist, who sat behind a Plexiglas screen. A computer print-out taped to the screen read "N.B: The receptionist CANNOT distribute petty cash or bus tickets. Thank you."

"I need twenty bucks, or they're gonna kick me out," one pleaded, pointing vaguely in the direction of the colony of rooming houses nearby, whose signs boasted "Rent by night, week, or month."

"I'll make you an urgent appointment with your case worker," replied the receptionist. It was the same answer he gave, earnestly, upwards of sixty times a day.

"Faggot motherfucker," the man muttered under his breath as he stormed out of the dole office.

Another took his place, saying sheepishly "I need bus tickets to get to an interview on Albion road."

"I'll make you an appointment..." The man interrupted him, "But the interview is in fifteen minutes!" he said, panic creeping across his brow.

Faced with this day-in and day-out, I was amazed that when the receptionist finally called my name my case worker so readily, even happily, hooked me up with 'assistance.' He took only a cursory glance at my neatly prepared paper work. We chatted pleasantly for a few moments before the next client arrived, somehow stumbling upon a mutual admiration of the architect Moshe Safdie.

After our talk died down he pulled something from the blue nylon lunch bag sitting on his desk. It was a red apple. He handed it to me, giving me a guilty smile. "My wife packs me one of these every day, but I never eat them. More of an orange man myself," he explained.

As I walked from his office, I peeled the sticker from the apple. I took the elevator down to the street and set out into it, traversing a streetscape rendered barren of pedestrians by the cold February wind. The sky was frozen a bright blue, and my teeth, exposed to the cold, stung as I ate the apple.

"Can I have my glasses back?" I asked. The fear that held me taut was slowly leaving me. The air held only the simple binary of money versus no money, as opposed to the more complicated electricity of hatred.

"Look," the muscle began, his voice surprisingly childish. "I'm sorry about this. We're cocaine addicts, man." He grabbed my mangled glasses off the pavement. "Have you ever done cocaine?" I shook my head as he handed me the warped glasses. "Don't ever touch that shit. It's evil. It'll fuck you up, fuck up your life." I wondered whether or not he was being earnest, until I realized it didn't matter.

As if sensing my disinterest in his sermon, he chose to illustrate his argument. "I mean, for example, here I am robbing you, right? Anyway, it's nothing personal. We just need a fix, we're addicts."

His partner came back across the street fuming. "You only had forty fuckin' bucks in your account!" he said in a nasal voice. "What the fuck? I thought you were in high-tech and shit," he said, no doubt referring to my faux Fred Perry shirt and twenty dollar khaki pants. Fuck it, I thought, this is the last time I dress respectable.

"Good thing your account has overdraught," he said, fanning a wad of twenty-dollar bills, as if he learned it straight out of any of the multitude of bill-fanning hip-hop videos he studied on his path to becoming a small time hood.

He grabbed my wallet from the muscle and tore through the few cards held in a clear plastic sleeve. "You don't have a driver's license?" he asked.

"I don't drive," I said.

"I want to find your fuckin' address," he said. A spike of fear drove through me as he looked at my health card, which had my address printed clearly on the back, if he had cared to look.

"Listen, you little piece of shit," said Rat-face, "you now owe the bank two hundred dollars, okay? You never saw us, you never saw anyone. I don't need your address, okay? I got friends, and if I get word that you ratted on us, me and my friends are going to hunt you down and kill you. Slit your motherfucking throat, okay? So don't even think about ratting to the five-oh."

No longer a hostage I walked the six blocks to the cop shop in a daze. The residential streets were torn up for construction, and I sat for a moment on a pile of gravel. I knew I would have to write a report for the police, so I tried to go over what had just happened in my mind, but my head felt like it was full of cotton batting, and the world seemed far away. I watched a series of cat eyes flickering on and off in unpredictable patterns the length of the quiet night street.

"I got buddies who tend bar down at the Gluepot," Matty said. "That's where those crackhead crackers hang out. Those motherfuckers are always bragging about their criminal pasts. So what I'm going to do is give you a beeper, and I'll page you when we finally find these two jackasses who mugged you." He continued to speak in an even tone. "Me and my buddies will take 'em out to the alley and you can watch us throw them around a little bit.

"Then, once they apologize to you. I will personally extract a tooth from each of their mouths with my bare hands. These teeth will be mounted on a ring, or maybe a necklace for you to wear." His arms, which he used to demonstrate his plan, hung loose at his side.

I took another sip of beer. "Wow, thanks."

"Alright everybody, we're ready for Thanksgiving dinner. You can all go and find the place setting with your name in front of it." My aunt Donna patted me on the back after her announcement.

I wandered into the dining room and found my place at one of the table's twenty-four settings. I sat down and watched my aunts, uncles, cousins, family friends, and ghosts slowly stream in after me.

(Ghost Pine #7: Blood, 2003)

SPRING

IT WAS SPRING AGAIN IN MY HOMETOWN. ARSON STALKED Ottawa; buildings in every corner of the city were going up in smoke. One moonless night a homeless man was thrown off the hundred foot cliff near Good Companions; the paper reported every bone had broken. At the city bus yards a mechanic, tired of being teased, took out his frustrations with a shotgun. When police arrived five bodies lay on the oil-stained tarmac, including that of the gunman. Ottawans were taking their post-cabin-fever dementia to the streets as never before. Melted from its deep freeze the city succumbed to a blaze of spontaneous combustion.

Faced with tumult, Ian decided it was a good time to clean out his back shed, sorting the useful detritus from the rusted debris. Somewhere in the rubble he found Grace, the real heroine of this story, always by my side, even when I don't mention her by name. There she was, still as slim, quick, and spry as her named implied. Ian looked her over, dragged her free of the rust pile, and gave me a call.

Ian was my student; he had but one class to finish before he could receive his diploma, the dreaded O.A.C. English. He tried to learn and I tried to teach him, but our weekly tutoring sessions imploded almost immediately and over something as petty as payment. See, he paid me for each session with one of the lukewarm 40s of malt liquor he always carried in his backpack.

"Okay, list three occurrences of the stone angel motif in Margaret Laurence's novel..."

Ian looked out my bedroom window. After the long grey winter the world was back, in bright greens and blues. "Do you want to drink those now?" he asked, pointing to his bag.

"Yes."

As Ian drank, his eyes glowed. Everyone was talking about them, green and deep. He hid himself in stretched-out shirts and under a black mat of hair, but his eyes burned through the dirt, pulling people in. He was the mystery everyone wanted to unravel.

That spring I was asked the same question so many times I lost count: "So who's your new friend?"

"That's Ian, from the West Side."

"He's got really nice..."

"Eyes. Yeah, I know."

"Is he...?"

"No. He's not half Japanese. Purebred Irish."

In the valley I'm from spring is barely a season. The clear, warm days are interrupted by freak blizzards which strike as late as June. Freak heatwaves hit as early as March. This year winter hung on and the fade into spring was heartbreakingly slow. Then one day I woke up to find stagnant air, a sky the colour of a dirty white t-shirt, and acts of violence and arson fading to the background. My hair began to curl; summer had arrived, earlier than expected.

Grace and I rode through the thick of traffic, escaping murderous automobiles. We biked downtown everyday, speeding through red lights at the height of rush hour traffic, and lived to tell the tale. Grace and I were never apart and I admit it, I loved her, still do in fact. Who cares if she's just a white ten-speed built for thirteen-year-old girls?

Summer days find suburban streets empty, vacant of all signs of life. Inhabitants retreat to their air-conditioned homes as the Ottawa Valley heat and humidity turn freshly-cleaned underwear into a fetid swamp upon going outside. Biking downtown I passed through Pleasure Park where streets swell and windows fling open. Hip-hop heads smoked dope and freestyled behind the community centre. Kids jockeyed for position on the crowded ladder of the slide. Across the street old folks relaxed, sitting in folding chairs on the lawn of their twenty-floor apartment tower. Arguing in French, Creole, and Hindi, speakers often switched from one to the other. Down the block, across from the convenience store, a policeman sat alone in his cruiser. Windows up, air conditioning on full blast.

"We were running around Mile End and damn if it didn't seem like the whole city was out. Hanging off balconies, drinkin' coffee on the patios." Robbie was getting whipped up just telling the tale.

"Then," Ian said, "We went to the park where they drum, under the mountain. Hundreds of people were milling around. Some kids built a huge bonfire out of burning trash. One guy started yelling 'Bring on the riot! Bring on the riot!' in French and then we all start yelling. A cop helicopter trained a spotlight on us, and then," he paused for effect, "Four city buses pull up filled with cops in riot gear, batons out!"

"And just like that," said Robbie with a glint of mischief in his eye, "Instant riot! People screaming, running into the woods, up the mountain, pelting the pigs with bottles. We barely escaped!"

I finally managed to visit Robbie in Montreal, and by the sounds of it, missed the best party of the year. This was a good thing, I consoled myself, since I came up for some peace and quiet. Ian was there for the same reason, but he had a knack for getting tangled up in things.

For the third year running tensions between him and his parents had boiled over. He left home, vowing never to return. Previous years he shaved his shaggy coal hair and retreated into the forest, where he abstained from all evil toxins and worked as a counsellor at a vegetarian summer camp hidden deep in the Quebec woodland. But this year there was no camp to run to. Depending on who you talked to, the owners were either taking a well-deserved break or fending off an audit by Revenue Canada.

This year it looked like Ian was in the cold cold world for good. He never got that high-school diploma.

If Ian's eyes were his most distinct feature then Chris's hands were his. Those big, freckled paws were always occupied: playing bass, driving his beat-up sportscar, drawing thumbnail portraits on napkins. But mostly he smoked, holding a cancer stick in his right hand at all times. He exhaled in my face.

"Our band has to start writing songs the way graffiti grows on bathroom walls." He paused to inhale. "Otherwise we won't get anything done. Naw mean?" We sat drinking coffee at midnight, tired and hyper at a diner in the suburbs.

Chris had been smoking since the age of twelve, and by now he was really good at it. We built conversations around his pauses. Discuss. Inhale. Stop to think. Drive the point home. Exhale in triumph. He used the orange tip as bullets, listing his thoughts as they were issued, rapid fire from his coffee enhanced brain.

Chris was afraid of heights so he waited patiently below as I climbed every access elevator in the neighbourhood. I explored flat pebble-topped roofs, finding walls covered in marijuana-inspired graffiti, always a pot leaf and an earnest 'Legalize It!' One night I stood in front of the supermarket air vents smelling the bakery's oven downstairs.

I thought seeing the old neighbourhood from high up would show me something new, but everything looked the same. Just because I was born here doesn't mean I should die here, I thought. Something had to change.

One day Robbie showed up, guitar in tow. He asked me, "Do you want to move to Montreal, live in my new place?"

I smiled and said, "Sure."

(Ghost Pine #6, 2001)

KILLING TIME

LESLEY SAT ON A CONCRETE BLOCK WITH HER LEGS CROSSED, brown dreadlocks hanging over her eyes. She talked hurriedly as her dispatcher's voice buzzed out of the radio duct taped to her messenger bag. She sucked in on her smoke. "It's good to see you back in town. Hey, I'm seeing a new boy, I think you might even like this guy."

"Is he human?" I asked skeptically, remembering the rogues' gallery of boys she'd dated. Boys with no teeth, boys who lived under bridges, boys with problems to say the least.

"He reads! I made sure to lend him some books and talk about them with him before I'd sleep with him. I just leant him *How to Make Love to a Negro*. He came back and told me, 'That's a fuckin' great book.'"

She pauses to take a call from the hub, a hot shot down on Elgin Street. Unlocking her bike she tells me "You should come over for coffee and apple latkes on Saturday morning. My boy might show up." On her bike, speeding off, she yells back to me, "He's so hot! He's got hair down to his ass!"

The money ran out and I was bitter. Stuck back in my hometown living in a tiny bachelor filled with dirty dishes and dusty novels. Ottawa was killing me in the same old ways while Montreal had been killing me in new, exciting ways. Starting with frost bite.

One day I put on my parka and walked through Centretown in the cold. My head was a mess. How could I stay in this broken dream town? I had too much history here, of pain, regret, and unfulfilled ambition.

I turned right onto Catherine Street and there it was: the bus station. I would spend my last twenty bucks on a ticket to Montreal, where I would rely solely on the kindness of friends and the free vegan lunches at the university for my survival.

It was a great plan, but completely destined to fail, so I walked right past the bus station. My destination was a squat three-storey building sitting under the Queensway three blocks up. A sign outside read Ottawa Art Bank, but once inside a plaque above the elevator read Social Services: Third Floor. Me and a few other hard luck cases got in the elevator, gulped hard, and pressed the button for the third floor. We collectively swallowed our pride and took the short ride up to the welfare office.

"My generation completely ripped you off. We went to school for free, smoked pot, and had unprotected sex. We snatched up all the good jobs and held onto 'em for dear life and now we expect you kids to pay for our retirement."

Sitting across the desk from me was a thick red-headed man

who looked like a former pro football player. I'd been dreading this conversation all week long, ever since I called Social Services and told them I had two dollars in my pocket and another five in the bank. But here I was and Bill my case worker was both begging me to take the monthly cheque "Just until you get back on your feet, of course," and apologizing to me for putting me in such a tight spot. Ten minutes after entering the building I was a welfare recipient of Ottawa-Carleton Social Services.

On the way home I ran into Jeremy on Bank Street. He was weaving down the road on his orange bike, thrown off balance by a suitcase filled with cymbals hanging from the right handlebar.

He was fresh back from tour and the road had left its mark all across his stubbly mug. This trip couldn't have come at a better time for him; it began the morning after he broke up with his girlfriend for good. Two weeks south of the border was just what the doctor ordered to cauterize his broken heart.

"I love it, life is so slow, drive all day, play at night..." Words failed him.

Last summer I was in the van too. We smoked a lot, and before it rained the moisture pulled up the thick smell of tobacco and coal from every corner. It became a tour diary; we could calculate the distances between cities by counting cigarette butts. From nightclubs to basement shows, we killed ourselves to kill time.

Driving west down the 401 one night, Jeremy took a long drag, then turned toward me and said "Imagine if we could see all the people who died on this road, just lined up along the highway."

For a brief moment the sun came out and we walked together down the road of sagging porches. It was an awkward shuffle, both of us trying to relearn the city's pace. The snow melted to reveal the dog shit, trash, and warped bike carcasses winter left behind.

(Ghost Pine #6, 2001)

GHOSTS, PT. 2

IT WAS ANOTHER NIGHT AT THE BAR AND WE WERE DROWNING the humid summer evening in a pitcher together before sleep and the next day's work. I was telling the ghost stories I'd collected over the years, and for once not the usual ghost stories about old friends' bands and lovers long gone and the regrets that went with them. No, I was telling real, one hundred percent true stories people told me when I asked them "Do you believe in ghosts?"

After Katie's mom died a sparrow followed her everywhere she went for a year. When she woke up it was outside her window, at school she'd catch glimpses of it outside her class, and at night it would sing her to sleep. Every day for a year, the same damn sparrow.

Katie didn't think it was spooky, and neither did I, until she found out a small part of her Russian heritage. There is an old folk belief that if someone close to your heart dies without a chance to say good-bye, they will return to you in the form of a bird, following you until you've grieved.

Since the age of thirteen Jon has been having out-of-body experiences on and off. Mostly off, for the last few years. For a while he forgot about them, or just thought of them as strange daydreams. That was until he dug a little deeper and found that out-of-body experiences are a big part of the spirituality of his Cree ancestors. His dad has had them too.

Everyone at the table eyes Jon as I tell the story. We all love local ghost lore, especially when it's about someone at the table. Jon blushes, never wanting to be at the centre of attention.

Jon's story ranks right up there with the supposed ghost that lives on the off-limits fifth floor of the Museum of Nature and that spooky burnt out house behind the bus station on Arlington. Years ago someone scrawled "this house is haunted" across the plywood boards where the door used to be. One by one we admitted we'd all been curious about that house, and too scared to explore it on our own.

As the night progressed we made plans for an expedition

to that haunted house the next week, but soon the next week turned into the next night. And then, as our curiosity grew and our beer money dwindled, we were making our path down to the moonlit haunted house.

Luckily I had one good story left for the walk. This one happened to Lucy's field hockey coach.

After a tournament in Vancouver the coach was driving some young field hockeyers back to their hometown in the B.C. interior. But first they had to pass through a treacherous Rocky Mountain pass.

It was a foggy night and the coach was driving maybe a little too fast for the bad conditions. All the girls were sound asleep in the back as the coach drove past the countless deer crossing warnings that littered the road.

Sound asleep, that is, until one of the girls sat up straight, screamed "Deer!" at the top of her lungs, and promptly fell back to sleep. The coach was freaked out, and even though she didn't see anything up ahead she pulled over to the shoulder to catch her breath. Seconds later, three deer climbed out of the forest and crossed the road.

Early in the morning they pulled into town and the girls in the back seat slowly woke one by one. Scream girl was the last to wake and, surprisingly, she had no recollection of her late-night outburst.

When they dropped off the screamer, her house was surrounded by cars and all the lights were on, despite it being the morning's wee hours.

That night her grandfather had died and her family had gathered to mourn. Her grandfather had died just minutes before the girl's outburst.

Soon enough we were walking down Arlington. Wait, did we miss it? We retraced our steps down the street and came to a freshly bulldozed vacant lot where the haunted house once stood.

We sat on the sidewalk, bereaved both by the haunted house's passing and our drunken plan's absolute failure. I laughed in the midst of our disappointment.

Sometimes, when it seems like everyone we've ever loved has skipped town for good all we have left are our ghost stories to share. And sometimes it seems like even the ghosts have moved out of this town.

(Otaku #5, 1999)

FAMILY

"JEFF, I MISS HIM SO MUCH," SHE POUTED FOR THE SEVENTH TIME in a row.

I looked up at her from where I had been sleeping on the floor until she kicked me awake. My eyes were still crusted over. She was sitting on her unmade bed wearing pyjamas with hearts and cartoon bears across the front, her hair shooting in every direction.

"Fuck you. I can't believe you woke me up just to tell me you miss your boyfriend!" Chris was visiting his sister overseas for a month and Jenn had decided to lose her mind over it. She was house-sitting a three-storey mansion and I moved in to keep her distracted. Luckily I wasn't alone; squatting rights were claimed on each room, until every habitable closet and crawlspace was occupied by a long-lost friend and I had to sleep on the floor of her room.

"You're sad," were the first words I spoke to Jenn. We met on the school bus in the sixth grade and she had the looks of a real morose child, a hangdog expression and big pouting lips that never crinkled into a smile. She sat next to me completely silent every day for the whole year.

"He's in Australia!" She frowned. "I heard a song on the radio that said 'in the land down under women glow and men plunder.' Now I don't just miss him, I worry about his loyalty."

"I miss sleep. Let's get breakfast."

She nodded.

Downstairs a seven-foot carrot top stood in front of the stove, every element burning red hot. Home fries with onions and mushrooms sizzled in separate pans, barley soup bubbled in a pot, and pancakes were singing on the griddle.

The chef wore nothing but light brown freckles, red scrapes from a bike accident on Preston Street, and a pair of bright yellow jockeys. "Breakfast!" he screamed, dancing around the room flipping flapjacks.

Richie was an old friend of Ian's from the hippie summer camp. When I met him he was doing time in Toronto in a collapsing house filled with anarchists and garden variety miscreants. He handed me a veggie burger in the crowded kitchen. "That," he pointed to my burger, "is why I never have to spend any of my hard-earned welfare cheque on rent. Ha!"

He cooked two enormous meals a day for the house, with food from the overflowing Food Not Bombs donation bin on the porch. Using his well-honed culinary skills Richie scored free lodging in a long series of houses; our temporary household was just the latest to fall for his charms.

As I ate I watched the wasps hanging outside the window, looking for someplace warm.

I looked at Jenn and thought of the night last month I showed up at her house uninvited. I rang her bell at four a.m. asking timidly, "Do you have any Polysporin?" Standing on her stoop the porch light revealed blood dripping down my neck, turning my t-shirt a dark brown.

"Oh Jesus." She dragged me into the bathroom to find gauze and I nearly fainted when I saw the left side of my chin hanging from my face. "You're in shock," she said.

Chris emerged from the basement. "Make him drink this apple juice so his blood sugar level doesn't fall. Change his dressing if it gets saturated," she shouted as she rode off to my parents' house on my crumpled bike. As we waited for my father to whisk me away to the hospital Chris paced. "Wow... shit dude. Are you... okay?" I gave him a big thumbs up, lying.

I'd fallen off my bike after hitting some debris in the road as I sped down the slope of a bridge at twenty-eight kilometres per hour. I skidded three metres on my chin and busted up my left hand. Then I got up and biked for forty-five minutes, swerving through the industrial park and crying the whole way. I only stopped at Jenn's because I knew she could give me something to put on my hand before I went to sleep.

Thirteen stitches and two weeks later I was repaying the debt. Trying to anyway. Jenn always called us The Family. Her and Chris and me. We stuck together when everyone else was sick of us. We bought each other drinks in a cycle, because we all were waiting on different pay cheques. We watched foreign films in our parents' basements. We drank coffee and read the paper, but mostly we blew smoke and drove around in Chris's car, aimless but together.

The only regular resident left at the house-sit was Noel, a small brown dachshund. He sat on my lap contentedly as I rubbed his head, listening to the night creep up on all sides, the cicadas dying down and the cars on Bank Street like a rushing river.

As summer turns to fall nights get longer and cooler, and the SuperEx comes to town. Some towns have carnivals in June or July, and they are full-on blowouts of adolescent abandon. Not so in Ottawa; the SuperEx is perennially referred to by newscasters and parents as the last chance for summer fun and thus becomes a grim wake for freedom and pool parties, fucking in parks and wasted days. As the midway arrives at Lansdowne Park kids are tormented with the realization that they still haven't taken ecstasy, felt up the girl they have a crush on, learned to pop an ollie, or done much of anything over the last seventy days.

The midway sits below the original livestock exhibition building, the cattle castle. Tilt-o-Whirls, double Ferris Wheels, and haunted houses are punctuated by overpriced cotton candy stalls, crooked ring toss, and ubiquitous blue port-o-potties.

For ten days in August the kids amass here, ending sordid two-month-long relationships (admitting later in the girls' washroom that it "felt like a lifetime") and having the worst acid trips of their young lives.

The fairgrounds were only a block from our adopted home. Every night we would arrive on the back patio with a bottle of something, but soon enough our conversation would lapse and the backyard would hush. The only sound was the kids down the block, screaming their guts out on the rides or in front of the main stage where reunited hair metal bands played to boisterous teens. Lame rock 'n' roll could be heard all across town as it reverberated off the low hanging clouds.

Of the three people I knew who lived in Montreal I found Richie first. He was freshly moved into his new apartment and we had a joyous reunion over salad. We planned our new ritual. Monday night was garbage night in the nation's most cultured neighbourhood, and we would go searching for buried treasure. Sifting through the trash of the Plateau I found some chipped bowls and a chapbook of Greek poetry. Richie only had eyes for lumber; all night we carried slats, flats and wooden wine crates back to his apartment over the jazz club.

"What do you think of my fancy new loft?" In his bedroom stood a five-foot-high platform for his mattress. It was assembled from at least half a dozen different shades of lumber riveted together, wobbling away from the crooked wall.

"Where'd you get it?" I asked as I stacked wine crates in a corner.

"I built it, duh." He had a hundred watt smile.

We dropped the last of the lumber and headed north to the all-night bagel shop. Richie led me into a small trainyard through a well-worn hole in the fence. We tore apart steaming fresh sesame bagels in the belly of an abandoned boxcar. The stars held formation, distorted by the September smog.

I started to tell a story but Richie cut me off with the wave of his hand. "Listen!" Far off, over the din of the highway we could make out the sound of drums, guitars, and trumpets. Richie sat still, transfixed by the city's singing.

(Ghost Pine #6, 2001)

THIS STORY IS CALLED 'MY LIFE'

IAN AND I WERE WOUND UP ON COFFEE AND BLURRY-EYED AFTER dissecting all the small things that make life bearable and the big things that make it intolerable.

All night I'd been trying to tell Ian my new story. It was all about how I grew up in the suburbs where I never talked to anyone, and the streets were always abandoned when I went out. No community.

Then the breeze changed and we talked about Ian's crush. Here's the latest update: they held hands on the beach and drank a bottle of vodka straight. The next day he waited by the phone for five hours before snapping, running for coffee and calling me.

I listened and then filled him in on part two of my story. All about how I grew up and went to a high school like all the others. But mine at least had a large contingent of like-minded freaks and most of them were in my grade nine gym class. We felt so alienated we hated anything that showed any bit of hometown pride. It was all an extension of nationalism anyways, or some other vague evil. Anyone who showed school spirit was at best a fascist brown-shirt, at worst a closet Nazi bonehead, like the ones we were supposed to beat up at shows.

We picked up Steve. He was all talkative, like he gets after work. He led us up by the old school and I told them the part in the story they already knew. I turned the corner, cut my hair short and went to shows at the punk house with Adam. I still felt alienated but I'd at least found something I wanted to be a part of.

As that summer played itself out people began to talk to me and introduce themselves as I hid in the corner. More people than had ever talked to me on the stupid abandoned suburban streets. Michelle and Pete both sold me zines, Jon told me he liked living in the country better than living in the city. Matt told me about his favorite record and the boys in the band told me they were too sick to shake my hand when I met them in the pizza parlor. Small acts that were so significant at the time.

Then Ian told me he doesn't like reading reminiscences. I nodded. "I like hearing about what's new. Sometimes when punk boys get together all we do is talk about the old days but they weren't even that fun! We went to punk shows, sat in the corner and were too shy to talk to anyone. We had to wait three years to meet the kids that sat next to us at shows."

Ian's right. It's funny how the past sometimes feels like it's more real than what's going on now. Us boys like to talk about what went down two years ago rather than what went on yesterday or our crazy plans for tomorrow.

A car drove by and pulled over. It was Pat and now we were four boys out on the side of the street yelling, jumping up and down and getting stung by bugs. Talking and spitting and feeling tough.

Then a carload of girls pulled up and the street party began. I asked Pat to turn on the car stereo. We needed a soundtrack to our conversation of bad jobs and how we all feel broken. How we're doing nothing as the world hits its highest pitch. As everything we've worked toward in the past years comes to fruition we're sleeping in.

Or maybe it was just me talking to myself again. Everyone disappeared and Pat drove me and Ian back to where it all started. I figured out the profound ending to my story in the backseat but I forgot it by the time I made it home. Some stories should never be written anyway.

(Otaku #4, 1999)

9

FORTY-EIGHT HOURS

NOW IT SEEMS NAIVE TO ME THAT THIS IS ALL I EVER WANTED: A table at the 'café culturel du Sud-Ouest' that plays bad Québécois pop hits, a cup of coffee, my journal, a stack of zines and a half-read paperback of Gorky.

This city was my own private mystery once. Everything was mine to decode and unravel, a life in miniature. Grace and I would explore all day long. Little Burgundy for thrift shops, Mile End for fresh bagels. Afternoons in the Westmount library or east to the Sunday night all-ages shows. Grace was my travelling companion and best friend. She was also a girl-style white ten speed.

I'd sit in the shade of turning trees, under the smog that hung across the city in summer's last days. I wrote piles of letters. I was my friends' foreign correspondent in the city of cobblestones, beat-up cathedrals and foreign tongues. When I decided to move to the city I knew only three of its inhabitants, plus a girl who might punch me in the eye. My only map had no street or place names, only the locations of public libraries. So I went to a new one every day.

It took me that whole season in an unknown city to forget about things like hometown, old friends and bad years. Watching the leaves change colour and feeling the warm wind sour to a cool breeze, I slept in late and spent my nights hunched over a too-small desk, back cramping.

Always alone, but immune to loneliness, the city and Grace were my mistresses. The burnt-out row houses of the South

West hinted at better stories than a friend could ever tell.

Now in the café all that time alone has finally caught up to me; even if I'm only away from my girlfriend for forty-eight hours it stings like weeks and weeks. Free refills don't fill up my loneliness anymore.

(Fuzzy Heads Are Better #8, 2000)

RED

TRUE TO HER NAME RED WAS A DYED-IN-THE-WOOL COMMIE. She said the town had made her that way and I could see it. The dotted line dividing the blue collar suburbs and the rich student downtown was anything but subtle. Neither were the town's twelve prisons.

When we met I was sick and on my way to the big city. She let me hang in her apartment while everyone else went to the Trasheteria. I listened to Red's James Brown record and wrote in my notebook. I brushed my teeth and washed my face and started to feel human again. She let me sleep in her bed but kept me up until four doing her Russian homework for a class that started in three hours. I gave her my critique of Marx and then we talked about failed romances and all the shows we were both at but never met.

The next day she locked me and Ian in her apartment and told us to make as little noise as possible. Her landlords lived right downstairs and were always complaining about the noise, even though they were always having the most raucous parties. Even the free are prisoners in jail town.

When Red finally let us out she took lots of pictures of me and we ate tofu together and I started to think that maybe she liked me too. My heart had an early spring thaw when five minutes after meeting me she gave me a gigantic Misfits sticker.

Three weeks later Robbie and I were on the Bronson on-ramp, thumbs out. It was my first time hitching and I was ready for anything. After half an hour we got picked up by a sympathetic yellow van. But the prospects for adventure (read: danger) soured when I realized it belonged to the band I'd travelled with the summer before. They were on their way west to play a festival and we were riding loft.

In two hours I was in a basement watching Red scream louder than the rest of the band, even with no mic. We headed downtown in a crew but lost it. It was a full moon Friday the thirteenth and Red and I were looking for tofu in prison town. Instead we ended up in the messiest record store and I found a copy of that Springsteen record I'd been looking for, you know the one.

We were up on the main drag, smiling. She asked if I wanted to stay at her house so we could read each others' fanzines and kiss. I laughed and admitted that it sounded like the perfect punk romance to me.

The rest of the weekend was spent running to and from the only three places to hang out in town. From the university lounge where Mike slept nights since he was homeless and could pass for a student (he never slept much anyway since he drank too much Cherry Coke) to the late night dorm room where we made up the code word "reading Marx" for kissing so we could talk about it in secret. And the house that used to belong to a Prime Minister that we broke into, down by the water.

Some old friends of mine were playing a show in town. It was at the shitty illegal coffeehouse hidden in a back alley. I thought a shady dive in that town would be cool but instead of being run by crusty punks or bank robbers as I'd hoped, the manager was just a weaselly yuppie who was too cheap to pay his server's fee and charged too much for his bad coffee anyway.

The weekend closed and she asked me to stay but I had a feeling that if the sun went down on me in a prison town again it'd be trouble. So me and Robbie walked down Division to the highway again.

We got picked up by Andy, a prison guard with a backwards Kangol and his dog, Lou. He gave us the lowdown on jailhouse tattoos, prison MCs and how to make hooch by filling a foot locker with fruit juice, sealing it up and putting it under the radiator to ferment.

He also told us that jail libraries are heavily censored and I realized that that's what would end up killing me if I was in the big house.

The last time I saw Red the summer was just beginning. It was her last trip to O-Town before heading off to spend seven weeks in a crammed hot van with four smelly boys. I was so jealous, she was roadie'ing for my favourite band.

We went to a punk show in the basement of the old convent, ate at the late-night Chinese place where, if you're lucky, you can find cockroaches in the food, and ended up on the hills above the city walking a nature trail. I drank a bottle of wine while she showed me her new red star patch and told me about the novel she was writing. It was all about bad sex and blowing up computers for global emancipation.

Eyes to the sky: it was another full moon, competing with the city lights below. From the lookout the city was at its most beautiful; the dark covered all the daily mistakes I obsess over.

We were at our most beautiful too. Porcelain-faced and wine-eyed, looking past town all the way west to the continent's end. Slowly spotting all the as-yet-untold stories that lay across it for us. Laying in wait for us to pass by on separate paths and dates.

On the way back to the car we got lost in all those plans that blind us. We made it out though, saying our parting words. I wasn't worried, I knew I'd see Red again; even if I never did she'd still made her mark on me: that red bruise on my neck, my first hickey.

(Otaku #4, 1999)

POLE TO POLE

IT WAS SPRING AGAIN AND AFTER A LONG WINTER OF DORMANCY the telephone poles were ready to sprout. They were delicate flowers; first a lone bud would appear on the weathered wood. But soon, as the days got longer, the poles were quilted with overlapping petals of paper in all sizes. It wasn't long until the whole city was covered in a new season's growth of posters, flyers, canvases and photos.

Everyone was anxious to show off the art they'd made over the winter to stave off cabin fever. This wasn't just art being pasted up, it was survival. We were showing that whatever doesn't kill us will only make our work more vital.

Sarah B and I wandered the streets, holding hands and stopping every five feet to check out a new piece of graffiti, abstract chalk art, political pamphlet, lost cat poster, or bizarre message scrawled in sharpie. Then we would analyze, critique and deconstruct them in the middle of the sidewalk as the whole city climbed over us, walking too fast to notice the gallery that had sprouted up.

It was especially amazing for us to see since Sarah and I had met and subsequently fallen for each other in the dead of winter putting up our posters, my stories and her abstract art together.

Every gallery needs a curator and Damien was ours. One night he took Sarah and I on a guided tour of the gallery's East wing (formerly known as Elgin Street). Damien pointed out every new piece of graffiti followed by biographical info about its writer, which he knew from having grown up with most of them.

Damien also pointed out that a few of our friends who had just graduated from photography at college had taken their left-over, imperfect photos, tagged their crew name "Violence Against Windows" on them and stapled them high atop the poles, way up in the city's clouds of smog, to prolong the time before erosion washed them away.

Soon enough urban erosion settled in and the petals of the telephone pole flowers began to be torn down by rain and the unappreciative city. But for two weeks of spring the city had sparkled and shone and held secrets down every alleyway and up every telephone pole.

And so too went our romance: torn down by forces beyond our control. The flowers she sent me wilted, the neon cupcakes she made for my birthday were eaten and now not even a single one of our posters has been left up to recall our spring together, dancing from pole to pole.

(Otaku #5, 1999)

SHADEMASTER LOCUST

I SAT IN THE RED CHAIR IN THE MIDDLE OF MY KITCHEN AND Jamie stood behind me, working quickly, snipping my hair. "It's really hard to let go of a character," he said as we discussed the play he just finished performing in. "I just need to realize that they're dead and I can't just go on living in them.

"Don't shake your head, hon." He straightened my drooping head. "It's such an intense process, mutating a piece of yourself until it becomes something on its own..."

"What's next?"

"Well, I've been having a lot of one night stands lately. It's funny to say this, but it's not always about the sex, y'know?"

"Hm-hm."

"I feel like an anthropologist studying these men I'm going home with. I almost want to take notes on where they live and how they treat me. It's natural, but true, that some of the most macho guys melt into the biggest sweeties. Some guys tell me their secrets, and some, I can tell, are reliving some past trauma." He nimbly worked the scissors across the back of my head.

"Watch the cowlick," I said.

"It's out of control," Jamie agreed, trying to flatten my unruly hair. "So yeah, lately I've been all about intense and brief closeness with people. I almost wish I could bring a camera to these guys' houses, just to document the lives that came into contact with mine. I see beautiful Polaroids of their lives developing before my eyes." Jamie's hands paused, as he shifted metaphors. "I want to string these nights together like pearls on a necklace. Tilt your head," he said, looking at the side of my head. "If you don't get the wax out of your ears soon you're going to go deaf."

"It's February, hygiene hasn't been a priority."

"Go steal some Q-tips from your parents' house!" He took a sip of bourbon from a mug reading 'Majic 100: great music for a great city.' I watched his hands. There are worlds waiting to be born in those calloused hands.

For as long as I've known Jamie, since we were suburban teenagers, I from the West and he from the East, he has been stitching things together. He works on and off as a costume designer for theatre companies; the last one gave him a twenty-thousand-dollar budget and a sewing staff of five.

"I don't know what I'll do next. Whatever makes me happy, I guess." He put down the scissors and gave me a little scalp massage to get all the small hair follicles out. As his fingers danced across my skull they began to release a world of memory.

It was winter, the one after high school when Jamie and I became best friends. We drank Jack Daniel's and fell asleep next to each other on the floor at a house party out by the airport. Waking up the next morning we crawled into the crystalline cold of another February day, and waited for the bus. "I think I'm getting arthritic," he said, feeling the joints of his right hand one by one.

Another night, this one in the spring, he came out to my parents' house. It was warm and quiet, save the occasional squeal of tires against the pavement or the bang of a junebug against a window screen. When I saw Jamie at my screen door, I knew what he came to tell me.

"Look," he said, after we climbed to the uppermost branches of the shademaster locust tree in my parents' front yard. "I drew this." Life down on the street continued, people put out their trash, walked their dogs and watered their lawns. No one saw Jamie pull a crumpled piece of paper from his pocket.

He handed it to me. It was an image of an angel in silhouette, except its wings were just as noticeable as a little pot-belly. It was a drawing of me. The pot-belly, acquired from excessive consumption of beer at the Dominion Tavern, was the defining physical characteristic of my post-adolescence.

"I'm in love with you, you know?" he said.

"There, I think it's done. Go look in the mirror." He shook out the black towel that had been wrapped around my neck and began sweeping the floor.

I walked to the bathroom, shaking my head. I looked into the mirror and smirked. There, onto my neck, fell my brand new mullet.

(Two Dollars Comes With Mixtape #1, 2003)

WISDOOM TEETH

IN THE TWILIGHT OF MY ADOLESCENCE I DATED A WOMAN FIVE years my senior. She had just finished a long education and I suffered her knowledge.

We mingled a winter of our lives. She won my heart through my stomach, keeping me fed with rich foods. At the table she continued to woo me. Risotto. Vegetables in Peanut Sauce (that approximated So Good). Stuffed Squash.

In between mouthfuls of food we enumerated our days' events. The stages that our daily drama treaded were as different as could be.

The government paid her a salary to look at Internet porn, read overweight Russian novels, teach herself to read kanji with flash-cards and be a stereotype of big G government inefficiency. She had skillfully fallen through the cracks of Health Canada. Her supervisor was a doctor / bureaucrat whose passion was not management but infectious diseases. He occupied an office two buildings away and rarely looked in on her.

My day was seven hours long and for each I was paid minimum wage. It was one sustained movement; I walked miles a day in the tiny alley of service, behind the counter in a Tim Horton's franchise. I controlled machines which brewed coffee, injected the coffee with cream, and injected sugary syrup into carbonated water. Worst were the grey lines of office workers I served, spackled by their day's hitherto lack of coffee. The best lacked all conviction, while the worst were total snotty assholes to me.

Dragging my aching corpse home across the Laurier bridge after work, the carrot pulling me forth was the night's twin promises of dinner and sex. In those animal days I insisted on climbing aboard my lover every night, or her climbing atop my shipwreck of a body. The warm shot of orgasm was the night's five second answer to the day's hours of labour. For a moment my veins were harp strings after the plucking of some lovely tune. And then total muscle relaxation. And then the sleepiness...

One night we went to her office in the thick forest of government buildings rising above the Lebreton Flats. On her computer we composed a resume so I could get a better job. On the way out she pointed to a squat building without any windows that looked like an electrical shed or telephone switch house.

"That's where they keep the government monkeys."

I laughed, but then she said "No, really. Health Canada bought all these monkeys to test various AIDS vaccines on. They've used them for their tests and now they don't know what to do with them."

The unassuming laboratory did nothing in the moonlight as we walked toward the Transitway station.

And her teeth. One day at work I had to clear it with my boss that I could take a half hour lunch break, rather than my usual ten minutes, if I stayed a half hour after my shift normally ended.

I took a cab to the dentist's office in the mall where my doped girlfriend sat waiting, her bloody inch-long wisdom teeth wrapped in gauze and held in a small manila envelope on the table next to her.

I grabbed the envelope and led her through the dentist's back door, into a cab and up the elevator to our apartment and into bed.

In the cab back to work I examined the ochre crust of blood

that dried on the roots of her wisdom teeth, before shoving them into one of the pockets of my backpack. I still have them.

(Two Dollars Comes With Mixtape #6, 2005)

THE PUNCH LINE

IT'S A JOKE BY NOW, ALMOST A WAY OF INTRODUCING MYSELF AT parties. Sitting in the kitchen of my new house with my roommate and her friends, my trip to Japan comes up.

"What did you do there?"

"Wait, wait, let me tell the story." My roommate Leila is insistent, then pulls back. "Can I tell the story?" she asks and I nod with a smile.

"Okay so Jeff was in love with this girl and she moved to Japan, but they stayed together. He saved up all this money to go over there and live with her," Leila pauses before telling the punch line. "He gets there and she dumps him on the train ride home from the airport!"

I don't bother correcting her one factual error: I was dumped the next night, not on the train. I chuckle.

"On the fucking train, man!" she shakes her head. "Can you believe that?"

I spent the whole autumn living in a one-bedroom apartment with Jif to save money. He was my boyfriend, but solely for real estate purposes. Upon discovering that two sketchy boys were sharing an apartment no bigger than a child's bedroom, the super threatened eviction. That's when Jif broke down, nearly crying and admitting our affair. "Not bad, huh? He never asked why we each had our own bed either."

"Yeah, good work," I said. Every dish in the kitchen was dirty, Jif's friend B dealt drugs off my bed and the cats chased each other over my face every night, but it was fine.

I had these terrible cramps that dug deep into my stomach like a corkscrew. I was going to see a doctor until I realized that the pain only came on the days I called her, on the other side of the world. The cramps were just a symptom of something bigger.

"I'm sick," she would say. "It hasn't stopped raining in five weeks and I have to bike to school and back every day."

"Why don't you take the bus?"

"I don't know what bus to take, or even who to ask," she scolded me. "This is *Japan*," she said, as if that explained everything. The worst part was that I still loved her.

When the corkscrew in my stomach dug too deep I went to the tavern alone, before my evening shift. At that hour only a handful of bearded skeletal men inhabited the wood-panelled bar. While they watched the hockey highlights on the big screen TV, I stared at the label of my brown quart bottle, as if it were some tool of divination.

I was a terrible drunk. I mean bad at being drunk, because the bottle couldn't help me to forget. I only remembered in sharper colour the woman I loved and the year we spent together. I also couldn't forget the distance between us and the gastrointestinal horrors that came with long distance phone calls which uniformly began with her whining, "I'm sick, it hasn't stopped raining in weeks." Months before, just after she left town, our phone calls began with hope and love, but over the autumn they soured, mutating into something else, some unidentified emotion.

Some drink to forget, but I drank to remember, and after the second quart I wandered off to work with a head full of memories banging about.

"I'm finally getting over that cold," she said, only two weeks before I packed up my life and flew to Narita.

"Oh, what happened?" I asked cautiously.

"Well, it got to the point where I would come home every night from teaching at school, cook myself dinner and then sleep until morning. One night I got so sick of feeling like shit that I just went to the hospital emergency room. I'd been sick for six weeks! So of course no one at the hospital spoke English but I just wouldn't leave until they'd dealt with me. Eventually, after four hours or something, a doctor figured out I had a throat infection and gave me some antibiotics. Actually, I probably had to pay for them but they couldn't explain to me in English, so I took 'em. They were probably just relieved to be getting rid of me."

"Why didn't you get one of the other English teachers who knew Japanese to go with you?"

"No fucking way! I just reached a point where I decided that no one could help me out of this mess. I'll only do things by myself, whether it takes forever or not." She paused. "Some things here are so impossible."

The corkscrew in my stomach dug ever deeper.

(Kiss Machine #4, 2001)

LINCOLN FIELDS

THE SUMMER I WAS EIGHTEEN I WAS REALLY LEARNING TO FUCK.

She lived in the neighbourhood. From my parents' house it was a ten minute walk up the roadway by the sprawling community college, past the suburban bus station constructed of red steel pipes and along a thin black path through one of my hometown's countless haunted green spaces. The path led past a brook that smelled of dead fish to a hole in a chain link fence. Across the street was her house. She sat waiting for me on the front step, cigarette in hand.

"Your nose is so straight," she often said with a sense of awe. "Paul's nose was broken so many times."

"I heard those stories," I said as her soft hand lightly traced its way across my face. From nose to cheeks to lips.

"He got beat up everyday in junior high. None of those fuckers in his band would ever stick up for him, they just ran from the jocks and left him behind." Paul was Nicole's boyfriend and the only person who visited her, other than her parents, during her stay in the psych ward of the Royal Ottawa Hospital the year before. She was full of meds, out of her skull, and Paul sat by her bedside every day after school. Paul was also my friend, until I betrayed him by receiving a rough hand job from Nicole a month before.

The night of the betrayal Nicole had led me into the woods and laid down a blanket for us to lie on, surrounding it in candles. "This one is for friendship—as the wax burns down all these little things come out of it and you give them to your friends," she explained as sparks flickered from her lighter. "See, here's a tooth." She dislodged a black plastic trinket in the shape of a molar from the melted wax and gave it to me. "I don't know you," she admitted, "but I'd like to be your friend." Her voice frayed.

She pulled a clear plastic container of strawberries from her purse. We ate them in silence. The stars shone through the smudged June sky and the city buses growled across the tarmac of the nearby road.

"I got scouted twice," she said. "To be a model. The first time was in New York City and then at the mall downtown."

"I can believe it."

Her smile revealed a mouth of perfect teeth. "That was back when I was anorexic. When I was fourteen." She clipped her words and fidgeted like an injured bird when she told me her secrets.

"Last week one night me and some friends were on the bus and there was this sketchy guy with bad breath sitting behind us. He kept telling us 'you girls are so hot.'" She made her voice sound deep. "'I'll give you girls a hundred bucks if you strip for me. If you show me everything.'"

"Creepy." At eighteen I didn't understand the lives of beautiful young girls. I didn't understand how they were both vulnerable and powerful. Nicole was beautiful—small constellations of freckles were sprinkled across her face, below her bleach blonde hair and azure eyes.

"Well, it was only sort of creepy. We were already drunk by then. We'd gone to the club where they never card us and we were wearing these sparkly dresses... So we stripped for him." She laughed. "We got off at Lincoln Fields and walked into the cherry blossom trees. He gave us each thirty bucks and we took off our dresses, our bras, and then our panties."

"Did he jerk off?"

"No, he just watched us. We stood there for fifteen minutes. It got kind of cold. He left and got the next bus and we walked home. I used the money to get my tongue pierced," she said, manipulating the stainless steel spike lodged in her tongue.

I saw her almost every night that summer, spending hundreds of hours in her bedroom. Nicole's parents barely existed, and when they appeared it was usually off screen. They certainly had no effect on the lives of two lascivious teenagers. One night I arrived at the door of their immaculately kept house and was surprised to find these near-imaginary parents actually home.

"Where are you coming from, young man," Nicole's mother asked, holding an empty wine glass.

"I was just visiting my grandfather at the old folks' home."

"That's just great," she slurred lightly. "We're always trying to get our kids to visit their grandparents." She almost clapped with delight.

Nicole's father was grey-haired and possessed the girth of a retired football player. He rolled his eyes apologetically. "We were just leaving." By the time their SUV pulled from the lane Nicole and I were rolling around naked.

Sitting on her bed post-sex she watched my penis shrivel from beneath her duvet. A slow breeze crossed the room, its walls painted a light girlish pink but now covered in coarse black and white photos and collages constructed from the pages of dissected magazines. Her floor was covered with cracked CD cases and empty packs of smokes.

"Do your parents know?" I asked. "About us?"

"Yeah, of course." She exhaled from a freshly lit cigarette. "They don't care." And how could they? What bargaining power were they left with after coming home one day to find their daughter with her arms flowing blood in the bathroom? Checkmate. They might as well let her stay out all night at raves and hope she doesn't do too much coke or ecstasy. Might as well let her skip school, buy her cigarettes on her bad days and not force her to eat when she says "I hate food."

Any weapon in the parental armory was rendered null and void by the almighty pale horse rider. Death waited patiently in the summer shadows for a chance to pass her razor blades or a surplus of sleeping pills and shepherd her into a heaven of the teenaged dead. With their passive parenting they realized something fundamental about Nicole that I never accepted—she was a mine field. That any wrong step I made could have meant death, and I was just dancing through.

We swam some nights, in the pool behind her parents' house. We were free from parents, free from gravity and free from time. We floated in the chlorinated water French kissing and feeling each others' flesh. We grappled, but in the water there was no friction. My skin and hers, shaved smooth, two teenagers submerged under the purple night sky.

(Ghost Pine broadsheet #1, 2002)

10

MOVIE REVIEW
(WITH SIMON): *X2*

WE SMOKED UP IN AN ALLEY BEHIND A COMIC BOOK STORE JUST north of Ste. Catherine. Simon smokes harsh Plateau shake that always catches my throat and sets me coughing. It's not the smooth Pointe St. Charles weed I'm used to, hydroponically grown by a single father saving up for a move to the South Shore to make a better life for his kid.

Simon cupped his hand around the joint, lit it, took his allotted three tokes and handed it to me. This was exactly how I pictured substance abuse when I was a kid, filled with fear that were I ever to 'take drugs' my middle class suburbia would instantaneously collapse into a Canadian approximation of Compton as portrayed in gritty Hollywood films and I'd dodge drive-bys on my walk home from school.

What had happened to my staunch 'just say no' stance of grades one through nine? Was I simply brainwashed by the fear-inducing Public Service Announcements that peppered advertising breaks of cheerful Saturday morning cartoons with grave images of body bags, peer-pressuring gang bangers and eggs frying in a delicious approximation of a brain's reaction to crack rock inhalation? Perhaps these ads, produced by Partnership for a Drug-Free America (a consortium of big tobacco and the makers of morphine) only served to steer children away from prohibited substances as long as they watched the Saturday morning cartoons. Sure, the four-to-twelve-year-old set contains the highest numbers of junkies, but in my shel-tered experience they were strung out on the highly addictive substances contained in McDonald's happy meals rather than crystal meth.

Smoking weed with Simon in an alley in a major metropolis, both of us filthy and unshaven, I'd long left the fear-mongering of the Partnership for a Drug-Free America behind. It could now be said of us that we were more on the (what must exist on a sticker clinging to a head shop's front door somewhere) Partnership for a Free-Drug America side of things, despite our abhorrence of oxymoronic (emphasis on the moron) 'weed culture.'

The Paramount theatre is second to only the Casino de Hull for brightest lit place I've ever been. The lobby is packed with jostling cineastes making a dash to the box office where teen-agers in matching shirts sell tickets by the thousands to rude and/or high customers. It was Simon's birthday so I picked up the tab before we embarked on one of the ten escalators that cascade through the former office building.

I was already pretty blazed by the time we fell into the sweet bucket seats that almost justify the absurdly expensive ticket prices. The lights dimmed and we watched the pre-preview ads with the true enthusiasm of the stoned for the banal. Mar-keting has reached such an apex of cultural power that ads for hair-spray and telephone companies have been given epic plots, Hollywood budgets and cinematic release.

After each odyssey in advertising Simon noted, "Strong choices, strong choices," as if the culprit for this poorly cu-rated selection of advertisements could be traced back to any one person with bad taste, as opposed to the small armies of production companies and the CEOs, presidents and vice-presidents of marketing who all have a hand in crafting these exquisite pieces of shit.

Next we witnessed one of those insane displays of computer animation (where the viewer travels the bloodstream of the protagonist, witnesses a time lapse shot of the birth of civili-zation and its subsequent destruction and travels across the universe into the centre of a supernova all in under three minutes) that serve as title sequences nowadays.

The actual movie began explosive as all hell. Nightcrawler teleports his blue ass all over the oval office, destroying the President's detail of secret service goons and getting close enough to kill G. Dub Bush himself before having an unfortunate pang of conscience.

Okay, perhaps the leader of the free world portrayed in *X2: X-Men United* was the stock nameless president Hollywood parachutes in to every movie instead of the fortunate son his damn self, but after enough consecutive Sunday afternoons marching with tens of thousands of other pissed off and stylishly dressed Montrealers, I cheered as the German Catholic teleporter nearly did what everyone wanted to: assassinate the president of the United States.

(The past few years' descent into one long dirge on American Imperialism was marked for me by an increase in drug use and time spent hiding in my room listening to the Dead Kennedys. At one Sunday anti-war march I hallucinated a wolf the size of a building walking down René-Lévesque with us. He cracked open a few levels of the CIBC tower with his haunches and ate a few bankers, winked at me, and then flew away into parting clouds.)

The film's two hours of incoherent subplots, terrible stylized dialogue and spectacular special effects washed over my drug-addled brain like the sea eroding beach front. When Simon and I emerged from the theatre my brain was toasted. Night had fallen and we parted ways in the Metro, waiting on the bridge overlooking both tracks to see whose train would come first.

(Ghost Pine #9: Bees, 2005)

The Ballad of Stu Rhubarb

IT'S IMPOSSIBLE TO SAY WHEN OR WHERE I FIRST ENCOUNTERED Stu Rhubarb. All I know is that he was everywhere during my late teens and early twenties when my white hot passion for hardcore punk rock was mellowing into a milquetoast acceptance of other musical genres. Stu was on both sides. I ran into him at hardcore fests in bland Midwestern American cities as well as during my brief stint as a roadie for Canadian indie-rock bands (before there was money to be made in such endeavors). Stu would unexpectedly appear at the furthest flung show, at the Apollo in Thunder Bay or the Boys and Girls' Club in Truro.

Stu is an asshole. Many of the aspects of his life remain shrouded in mystery, but that fact is clear. He complains to no end about the slings and arrows of outrageous fortune that have assailed him. He has never had his name on a lease, possessed a credit card or, he swears, even had a bank account. After years of non-stop travelling he seems to know everyone everywhere and won't hesitate to say a bad word about any of them—even if they put him on the thanks list in their band's record.

Stu and I have been pen pals for years, sending letters in between our PO boxes. Despite the bilious nature of his correspondence, almost solely concerned with detailing how the town he was staying in or the band he was touring with sucked, I always enjoyed his bittersweet prose. Last year, after not hearing from him for over six months, I cracked open the shoebox filled with the letters he wrote to me over the last decade and remembered just how entertaining his writing could be. I wrote him a postcard offering to put out a special issue of *Ghost Pine* dedicated solely to collecting his letters. Not only did he decline my offer, but the postcard he sent me went out of its way to tell me, in no uncertain terms, how much my zine sucked. He wanted nothing to do with it.

So I wrote him back and called him on his shit—in all his years of complaining about bands and zines and poorly promoted concerts he had never had the guts to play in a band, write a zine or put on a show. Two weeks later I received my response, not in the form of a letter, but via Stu himself, who I found standing on the stoop of my apartment when I got home from school one day. He wore a beard, carried a sleeping bag, and had a utility belt strapped around his middle.

"Fuck you, man," he said as he moved into the closet of my apartment. "I'm going to write the epic-est zine the scene has ever laid eyes on. I've got incriminating stories about all the hottest bands of today," were his last words to me before he closed and locked the closet door behind him.

I didn't see much of Stu during his six week stay, I just heard the occasional cackle from behind the door. I offered him a spare computer we had lying around, but he refused it, screaming "No computers! Hand written!" and then lay back down on his sleeping bag, scribbling in tiny handwriting under a bare forty watt bulb.

Eventually the cackling from the closet ceased. It was replaced by mutterings and then silence. One day Stu was gone, along with my change jar and a pair of my jeans. He left only a small stack of paper—a fragment of his intended epic zine. It was some months before my school work calmed down enough that I could read it. I found myself laughing immediately and knew that I had to publish these stories. In typing them up I recognized that I was betraying his vision, but his handwriting was so tiny and dense that I could only read it after ten years of practice.

I collected and published Stu's stories under the name *Crud #1*, except for the vengeful diatribes against the bands that have employed him as roadie. Stu has never had any luck with money and to have him blacklisted from his one occasional form of employment would be, I think, a poor choice, one that would no doubt set him on the path to actual homelessness and alcoholism rather than the romantic punk rock variety that he has been toying with for the last several years. His PO box had since closed, so I invite fans to contact him through mine.

(Ghost Pine #11: Crows, 2007)

CRUD #1

FRIG THE COPS, PT. 1

BACK WHEN CHLOE AND YANNICK STILL MADE POSTERS YOU COULD read they were also prone to throwing little barn-burners down in their Old Montreal loft. That space was painted from floor to ceiling with alternating orange and purple stripes and stacked to the tits with posters, books, records, broken photocopiers, paint cans—you name it—and no less than ten cats.

Now, although C and Y dress in the manner of flea-bitten junkies and play in a degenerate noise rock band, they're actually health nuts. Straight-edge vegans, even. So at their parties there was always a spread of veggie sushi, vegan pâté, watermelon and various other treats cooked or cut up by C herself. After slaving in the kitchen all afternoon making appetizers for her pals C was still ready, willing and able to get the party started.

This one night in particular, C waited until the room was full of grotty punks and garden-variety weirdos before she ran to the stereo, threw on "Human Fly" and then lit up the dance floor in her living room, shaking like she was on fire. The party was on! As soon as the song was over she threw the record onto the floor and a fresh side was on the turntable. By the time there was a knee high pile of vinyl on the floor I had consumed enough Fin du Monde that I was literally swinging from the rafters.

The party was hot and sweaty. Fuelled by sushi and freaky rock 'n' roll it felt like there was nothing we couldn't do. I had a lovely lady on my arm that night, so when she suggested that it was time for us to start a smaller party in her bedroom across town I couldn't resist.

One problem: the bathroom was occupied by someone who just wasn't coming out and my bladder was full up. No problem, thought I, Old Montreal has been no stranger to piss—each of the centuries-old cobble stones have been sodden in the warm yellow liquid of a drunken idiot countless times.

On my way out I fell down a flight of stairs and got up feeling fine. Tonight I was beer-vincible! Or so I thought.

I was wrong. As soon as I found a patch of wall and un-zipped my fly I heard the whirr—the *Jetsons*-like sound of a Montreal Police minivan pulling up behind me. Once I was pissing I wasn't going to let a bunch of *flics* stop me. My golden stream persisted for another full minute before the pigs could ticket me.

I would never pay the fifty-five buck fine and the sympa-thetic gaze of my lady friend told me that she would soon do everything in her power to help me forget the asshole pigs of the SPVM. Nonetheless, "Frig the cops," said I.

PUKE STORIES: BUSES
PART ONE: HALIFAX TO TAMPA
Trains, planes, automobiles: all of these have escaped the bub-bling river of puke that has streamed forth from my mouth over the years. Boats and buses, especially buses, have not been so lucky.

For the first years of my perpetual travels I prided myself on possessing an iron-cast stomach. I could eat the fieriest dishes a subcontinental buffet had to offer, wash it down with gas sta-tion coffee and a fifth of the cheapest whisky before riding a bus down the winding-est roads for twelve hours without even getting so much as a mild case of the runs. Or so I thought...

I christened my puking career on a bus from Halifax to Tampa. The eve of my departure from Nova Scotia's capital had been spent drinking dollar beers at the Split Crow down in the Historic Properties. A Celtic band played shitty tunes as my old friend Sarah and I got sloshed. The place was packed with jocks, among them Sarah's sister, who greeted me as if she knew me and then proceeded to call me Scott or Shawn or Don. Whatever.

With Caleb's help we stumbled back to Parker Street, where I slept for a good two hours before getting up to meet the bus. As the Hound crossed one of those big bridges in the early morning light, I looked down upon all the cars outside the window. Ha ha! You fools, going to work!, I thought. I'm young and free! I'm totally puking all over myself!

Luckily there was almost no one else on the bus and I could get myself back to the bathroom before puking the mother lode into the chemical toilet. Walking back to my seat, I smiled. I may be a moron, but I do know that puking is a lot better than not puking. I learned that lesson after drinking a bad banana milkshake in Bangkok.

That said, the puking lifestyle is not without its victims. On our smoke break in Moncton, I went to the bathroom to splash some water on my face. Looking in the mirror I noticed that my prized (Young) Pioneers shirt was covered in drying patches of vomit. I was going to be on the bus forever and couldn't exactly stow it in my bags with the rest of my clothes.

So I got out a clean shirt and pitched the YP shirt in the bathroom trash bin. I shed a tear or two for my old T as I walked back to the bus.

PUKE STORIES: BUSES
PART TWO: BRANDON, MB.

I have fond memories of my first trip to SF. Living on a rooftop with Myles and Alana, with the whole city glittering below us. But as they say, the journey is half the fun, or something. Alana missed out in that regard. She flew and met us there instead of taking the seventy-three-hour bus ride to Vancouver where some friends of Myles's were picking us up and driving us SF-ward. A shady plan, for sure—but it worked!

Myles was a few years younger than me, which I didn't realize until after a few years of knowing him. This was his first big trip and, appropriately, a white hippie with a faux-Jamaican accent sat behind us the whole way. On a break in Sudbury we walked across the street to the bowling alley and ordered beers. We were the only two people in the place but just as soon as we received our bottles of Blue the lights went out, the disco ball went on and the thump of Euro-beat blasted from the speakers. It was four p.m., but for us Rock 'n' Bowl was starting early.

Anyway, you get the picture, and lest we forget that this is a *puke* story, not a *bus* story, I'll get on with it.

So there we were, in Brandon, Manitoba. The bus stopped at midnight for a smoke break. Myles had had a hard time sleeping ever since the day before when he woke up to find his face in my crotch and the nearby hicks giving him the stink eye. To calm his nerves on the eve of our second bus night he pulled out a bottle of rye from his bag. We bought a fountain drink from the snack bar and poured an indeterminate amount of booze into it. Drinking it down in no time flat, we passed out instantaneously. Two hours later I awoke totally nauseous; Myles was asleep in the aisle seat and could not be roused. As the bus rolled on I resigned myself to my fate of puking all over myself once more.

I felt it creeping up my gullet when I noticed the empty fountain drink cup in the garbage bag beside me. I fished it out just in time and puked right into it, as quiet as could be. A whole lotta puke came out—I was worried about spill over —but it stopped just below the brim. Thank god we got a large pop!

I put the top back on the cup and very gingerly placed it back in the trash bag. I looked around the crowded bus—all the lights were off and everyone was asleep. It was the perfect puke. I patted myself on the back and promptly fell back to sleep. An hour later we pulled into the next rest stop. I took the cup and dropped it into the first trash can I passed and then went to the bathroom to fill my water bottle.

FRIG THE COPS, PT. 2

A mllion years ago it was still legal to be a squeegee kid in Toronto. Unfortunately in the nineties that royal pair of knobs known as Mel Lastman and Mike Harris teamed up to make it a capital offence.

The punks were not happy and neither was OCAP. At the end of the big Active Resistance Anarchist Conference we filed out of Symptom Hall and over to the 52 Division of the Toronto Police to protest the criminalization of being poor.

There was a huge turn-out. University was blocked and at least a thousand or two royally pissed protesters surrounded the station making a hell of a lot of noise. To this end organizers were handing out noisemakers: a stick, a nail and a few tin can snippets. I got my hands on one and proceeded to get as much of a racket out of it as I could.

It wasn't as big as the march on Queen's Park where police horses trampled protestors and Maggie saw Billy Bragg walking around playing guitar and wearing an amp on his back, but it was still a pretty big hoo-haw and it felt good to blow off some steam. This was pre all that Black Bloc stuff however, so only a few newspaper boxes got tipped, no flipped cars or anything like that. The fortress of Div 52 was unassailable, a Helm's Deep of concrete and reinforced glass brick.

After the howling was over I made the mistake of sitting with Chad on the empty sidewalk. He was no protester, just a passer-by. I still had my little noisemaker in hand when an unmarked minivan pulled up beside us and a cop dressed in full Darth Vader-style riot gear and wrap-around shades jumped out of the passenger side. He wrenched the noisemaker from my hand and threw it to the ground, stamping on it with his jackboots like a child having a tantrum. Only once it was completely crushed did he see fit to jog back to the van and squeal out onto the mean streets he had vowed to serve and protect.

Chad and I laughed for a long time but in between peals of laughter I managed to choke out "Frig the cops!"

(Ghost Pine #11: Crows, 2007)

HASHISH IN CALGARY

*I was incapable of fearing future misfortune, future
solitude, for hashish would always remain.*
Walter Benjamin, "Hashish in Marseilles"

WE PARKED THE VAN IN THE ALLEY AND LOADED AMPS AND
instruments downstairs into the club. We put them on the
stage and retraced our paths to retrieve another armful. Like
every other day, this one had begun with hours spent in the
van and it felt good to stretch our legs.

Our only ritual in the van was collectively working on the
Globe crossword until it was done, first thing every morning.
We also read books, drank coffee, talked, and tried not to get
on each others' nerves. Keeping the peace was essential as the
six of us were rolling across the country in cramped quarters.

When all the gear sat in a corner of the stage, we rubbed
our sore hands together. The show would start in a few hours
and in the meantime several of our number dispersed, going
for walks alone or looking for payphones or Internet cafés in
order to connect with home.

Jon nodded to me and then the door. He held the pink box
containing the small chunk of hash his brother, a pot farmer
in Northern B.C., had driven halfway across the province to
deliver to him in Kelowna the night before. In the few moments since load-in Jon had already been to the bathroom and
rolled a bit of brown gum into a joint and tucked it behind his
left ear. He led me outside.

As I smoked, the alley was flooded with sunshine. It illuminated the green dumpster, the sagging power lines and the
tags that covered every wall.

I stepped outside of time for a few moments, retrieving the
few memories I had of this city. One in particular came to me:
sitting on a park bench across the street from an elementary
school during a bus layover, going home after my first time
travelling alone. I watched the school children playing and
had the dreaded realization that I had no idea what was going

to come next in my life. But it was not dread alone, it was married to a strange wonder at the endless possibilities that lay ahead. Now that same feeling began washing over me, and yet the hash kept it at bay, insulating me for a moment.

"Calgary," was all I said to Jon. It seemed to me that the name of this city perfectly described the feedback loop of memory I was living through. "Fuck," I punctuated.

He nodded with a deep knowing. The night before he had introduced me to his own brother as his "brother from another mother."

The joint was gone, but it had worked to slow time and stretch our moment of togetherness into a fortress unbreachable by the future. Even the September breeze was stilled.

My bones felt light. I laughed.

We were far from home.

(Ghost Pine #10: Wires, 2007)

11

ON THE ROOFTOPS
OF SAN FRANCISCO

THE FIRST TIME I VISITED SAN FRANCISCO I STAYED IN A TENT ON A roof in Potrero Hill. Myles's old friend was one of the thirteen Irish university students who lived in the apartment downstairs. They all had visas to work in the States for the summer and slept on rows of air mattresses.

There were two rooms, one for each gender. The 'lads' room smelled faintly of urine because Paul, the sole Brit among the Irish, drank until he passed out and pissed the bed every night. The students were squares and yet lived in conditions far shittier than even the most claustrophobic of punk houses. They had all of the squalor but none of the culture.

One night Billy Joe, a recent transplant from Tennessee whom I had met a few nights before on the roof of a parking garage, came over to check out my strange living situation. After a crowded spaghetti dinner in the kitchen we retreated to the roof, where we drank from cans and stared out at the city. We could see all of it, jewelled hills climbing and falling in every direction to the end of our vision.

Billy Joe said, "Y'know, people save for years to buy a house on this hill with this view. But once they move in they have to work every goddamn day of their life to pay down their mortgage. They stop looking out at the city and forget what they moved here for.

"It's only you and me who can see this shit for its beauty, because we didn't pay for it. We stole it."

                                    (*Ghost Pine #10: Wires, 2006*)

THIS NEVER HAPPENED

LAST NIGHT AT THE STORE MANNY LEFT THE BACK DOOR open to let in some fresh air. Around eight p.m. we heard the yammering roar of a crowd echoing up the walls of the alleyway.

"What the?" Manny peeked out the door and then waved me over. "Dude, you've got to check this out."

In the alley forty teenagers all dressed in the same yellow T-shirts stood drinking cans of beer.

"What the fuck is this?" Manny asked. Two people stepped forward, coming up onto the loading dock to talk to us. "Why are you drinking *here*?"

"Because it's off the street," a blonde girl with an orangey tan replied. Her eyes sparkled with shiny makeup and her jean cut-offs revealed legs that had been shaved or waxed or lasered free of hair.

"Please don't report us." Her male cohort, a square-jawed former high school athlete threw himself on our mercy. I snickered, not having heard the word 'report' used in that way since elementary school when it was a threat bandied about the school yard.

"So what's in it for us?" Manny asked.

"A beer?" the girl offered.

They handed us each a warm can of Molson Ex and asked our names.

"Uh, Jeff," Manny said, taking my name.

"I'm Emanuel," I reciprocated, taking his.

"Greetings Jeff and Emanuel!" the two dozen kids shouted at us and then recited, not quite in unison, a bawdy limerick.

"Now chug!" The blonde girl commanded.

"Are you kidding? I'm not going to chug, I'm at work!"

As we held the warm beers ("What, they got a fat kid to put

these in his armpit all day?") a brazen freshman climbed onto the loading dock, found a corner and began to piss, his urine streaming down into the storm drain.

"Aw Jesus," I said, as we left our unopened cans by the door.

"Dude," Manny said, "Just forget about it. This never happened." I followed him through the door and pulled it shut behind us.

(previously unpublished, 2008)

SCENES FROM A TRAILER

"I'M THE KING OF DALHOUSIE!" IAN HAD BAGS UNDER HIS EYES as he explained his work schedule. "I work at the coffee shop from six to midnight then I head next door to the pita place where I serve drunken jocks until four a.m. It seems to me the bigger the asshole the more mayo they want on their pita."

"Between my two jobs I manage to keep all my friends caffeinated and fed, and I only work sixty hours a week! I've got to open the coffee place at seven so I'm not even going to try to sleep." My watch read 5:30 a.m.

Ian pulled something out of his pocket. "Want a wake-up pill?"

"Okay."

He popped two of the purple caffeine pills then handed me the package. It had a crowing rooster printed on it. I dry-swallowed a pill and handed them back, but Ian was already asleep in my orange armchair.

The trailer was a mess of lighting gels, Victorian props and costumes, a small PA system and Ian asleep with a string of drool creeping down his chin. He had been my main contact with the outside world since I started this job.

I spent every night of the week in the trailer. I was paid to watch the stage, bleachers, and lights set up outside in this park by the river. This was 'Theatre Under the Stars,' and I was the night watchman. Past midnight it got so quiet that all I could hear was crickets, bull-frogs and the wind through the trees.

"Oh shit, I'm really starting to feel it!" James visited every couple of weeks, always on a different drug. He had just taken ecstasy and was frantically walking around the stage. He walked into the trailer and put a house CD on the stereo.

Seeing people out in the park in the middle of the night was always interesting. My friends were out of sorts and always showing their frayed edges. If they were tired I'd make a bed out of seat cushions and give them my sleeping bag. If they were exasperated they could come and sit in silence for a while, and if they wanted to talk we could do so for hours without interruption.

"I'm worried that I'm never going to fall in love. I just turned thirty-one and everyone I grew up with is getting married and having kids, even my ex-wife," Mike lamented as he beat me at Scrabble.

"I miss the sea. Should I stay in Ottawa or sail around the world?" Pixie asked.

"Me and Jenn are breaking up! I need a new apartment! And a new bed!" Chris told me.

"I don't think I can go to Bolivia! The ambassador's on vacation and I can't get a visa until he gets back," Bethany fretted.

"I'm starting to think nuclear holocaust is going to happen sooner than later," JB predicted.

Everyone came to me with their big dilemmas and my response was always the same. "Do you want some water? I could brew a fresh pot of coffee. Let's go sit by the river and watch the swans."

At four in the morning nothing seemed too pressing.

I sat outside on the highest bleacher, the sun beginning to blur the horizon. The adrenaline of beating another night into submission coursed through my veins. The park was covered in dew and the joggers had yet to emerge. The trailer door opened slowly and Ian stumbled out looking even more tired than before he fell asleep.

"The sixty hour work week is killing you," I said as I climbed down.

I gave him a hug. He strapped on his bike helmet and coughed, "We've got to stop meeting like this," then pedalled out of the park.

(Ghost Pine #10: Wires, 2006)

MIDNIGHT REVIEWS

I.

HERE'S WHERE IT BEGINS: ME AND SARAH B. ON OUR HIDDEN rooftop hideaway. We hopped the fence and scaled up the yellow pipes to find our oasis in a sea of Saturday night drunks. On busy nights we watch our friends come and go from the diner across the street. We are Saturday nights spies and oh, please don't drop by for a visit.

Up here I try to tell Sarah the stupid little stories that I've collected over the years, ranging from Greek mythology to punk hagiography. I want to tell her big scary truths rather than just these small stories.

But all I can manage is the tale of Orion and the scorpion he once killed, only to have it follow him across the winter night sky forever.

She laughs, wondering what I'm getting at.

The story is up there, even as the constellations are dimmed by the city of light bulbs.

II.

Out in the western suburbs the stars aren't much brighter. Our makeshift family, Chris, Jenn and I, sip Sleepytime tea on my slowly rotting deck and under the rapidly shedding canopy of the Russian olive tree.

Sipping our tea in the dark, the silence is dented only by the humming chorus of suburbia: backyard pool filters, air conditioners and the odd squeal of car wheels coming from Meadowlands three blocks to the south.

We sip our last few minutes of night before we head to our beds scattered all over the neighbourhood. In the morning

Chris heads to work in the dishpit at Briskets, Jenn's off to finish high school, and I've got another tour group to lead.

Midnight, and in this neighbourhood our eyes are the last to close.

III.
Driving home from the show I tell Jeremy to pull over.

How many times have we driven down the 417, commuting from one concrete mess to another, but never stopping to see its best roadside attractions? Not the truckstops or doughnut shops, but the tall crooked pine trees and the clearings of long-grasses and wild flowers.

We'd just shared our night with a basement full of four hundred smelly kids bouncing off the walls and vying for the best spot to watch the band from.

Four hundred is not a bad head count for a medium that turned alienation into an aesthetic, but now let's pull over and experience one of the few things shared by all: the midnight canopy. Let's pull over and stare down the stars, they're brighter out here than in any city. Let's pull over and rename the constellations one by one!

He declined, citing the fact he had to work in under five hours at his government job. So instead we just watched the falling stars and the red light radio towers that litter the sky.

IV.
At midnight I slipped out of my cabin and into the lake, swimming across the bay to the small anchored raft.

The stars shone the brightest I've ever seen them. As the breeze dried off my skin, the waves sang in harmony with the bullfrogs of the swamp and the dancing trees ashore.

(Otaku #5, 1999)

MILLENNIUM

A HUNDRED FACES, A FEW FAMILIAR, APPEARED AND DISAPPEARED down the halls of Ian's house. You never feel as warm as when sitting by a heating duct after spending the better part of evening with your face buried in snow. Cat talked rapid fire to me about her new life at school in the big city, Richie played DJ in the corner, and Jamie and Eric made out on the couch.

Ian's birthday fell on the last day of 1999 and everyone had dressed up nice for the end of the world. Paranoia about planes falling from the skies, computers evaporating, and markets imploding were rampant. Now we were into the last minutes of the year, a few people turned on a TV and counted down "5...4...3..."

Adam tapped me on the shoulder. He had just arrived and didn't know a soul at the party, so he made a bee line for me and my bottle of rum. I hadn't seen him since Christmas Eve.

I don't know how, our Christmas tradition started, but we follow it every year. We start late, drinking a beer each in my parents' living room. We watch the same movie as last year, about heavy metal and murder in a hick town, until we start to get antsy.

Driving downtown our faces are lit by the glowing digital radio station call numbers.

We arrive at the diner and mumble "Coffee and fries" to a waiter in a dirty t-shirt. Christmas Eve is the only night of the year quiet descends on the diner. The stereo is off, to eerie effect. The buzz of the neon signs is audible, as well as the bubbling of the deep fryer in the kitchen. The wind howls down the street, testing the strength of the window panes.

"There's this kid who owns all this land outside of Portland. Punks go out there and camp for months at a time. I might do that for a while after I get my degree, or go to grad school," Adam said.

"Most of my contact with the pepper spray at the APEC protests was indirect. I didn't get any in my eyes." Or "We just got evicted from this old hospital we were squatting with two hundred homeless dudes." Or "I saw D.O.A. play in Jen and Andy's basement!" This was how his infrequent letters began. After high school he had moved to Vancouver and unwittingly arrived in the middle of a war against all things halfway decent. Adam's letters offered sketches of the people and punk houses of the Pacific Northwest; scene reports of kids trying to eke out a bit of freedom in the land that invented the three dollar cup of coffee.

But as vital as those letters were they couldn't hold a candle to the tales he delivered in person, clipped monologues of the struggle spoken between drags off of cigarettes and sips of black coffee.

"I was in Bellingham, checking it out. That town's full of ruins from its days as a mill town. But, shit man, it surprised me how far the yuppie thing has gone. Every empty warehouse had a sign up for new condos or offices for Internet companies. I'm all for urban renewal, but that shit is just so lame. I mean, what does it leave us?"

The nineties, three dollar coffee, Internet everything, 'loft style' condos. The nineties spread like an ink blot into an ocean, reminiscent of wartime news reels charting Nazi progress across the nations of Europe.

"Yeah, shitty," I offer.

The policemen eating poutine by the window stare out at the empty street. Imagine it as something out of a post-apocalyptic film: lights blinking yellow, red, green to empty intersections. For hours at a time the only traffic is snow dancing across the road, the cars completely buried.

The hands of the clock align. Midnight. A tired, solemn chorus of "Merry Christmas" wafts across the room. The lights are still too bright, the red vinyl booth still painful to sit in and Adam asks me again, brows furrowed with thought, "What's a guy gotta do to get a refill around here?"

(Ghost Pine #6, 2001)

12

CIGARETTES

WHEN MY GRANDFATHER HARRY MILLER PASSED AT THE AGE OF ninety-one I was living in a windowless room a block from the funeral home. The night he died I went to see his body at the hospital with my dad. Later Jon bought me a bottle of wine and we sat on the fire escape for a long time drinking and smoking cigarettes. It was May and the sun hung in the sky long into the evening.

The Hulse, Playfair & McGarry funeral home is so pristine that as a child I aspired to live there. Although it stands only one storey tall its operations extend deep into the soil, with two basements of embalming rooms and cold storage. The walls are thicker than those of any house I've ever been in, successfully muting the sound of chatting mourners.

For three evenings in a row my extended family gathered in one of the home's parlours at six-thirty and chatted amongst ourselves as we awaited the throngs of callers. Our sorrow was surpassed by our bemusement at the strange custom in which we were participating. The script went like this: we, the bereaved, were to mill about, making pleasant conversation with visitors who had come to pay their respects to the departed. They spoke in stage whispers, each one uncomfortable discussing the subject of death. Inevitably they took a peek at the corpse, signed the guest book and left discreetly. Nothing that took place inside the parlour's beige walls had anything to do with death or life; it was a place outside of time.

The last time a relative had died I was fifteen and sullen.

Rather than staying in the parlour I explored the rest of the funeral home, eventually finding an empty lounge where I sat reading *The Basketball Diaries* for hours at a time.

By the time my grandfather's death came around I had grown up enough to accept that it was my responsibility to suffer through the wake with the rest of my family. Most of the time we were tired and bored, waiting for the public display of grieving to be over with so we could finally go back home to our lives.

I had a secret that got me through those visitations. It was stuffed into the inside pocket of my thrift store suit. The night my grandfather died I bought my first, and only, pack of cigarettes. Every day on the short walk to the funeral parlour I would suck a few drags. As the cigarette burned, I imagined all my frustrations with the stage-managed grieving process and the old family animosities turning to smoke along with the tobacco. I felt sheer joy in knowing that with every puff I took I was a little closer to death.

(Ghost Pine #9: Bees, 2005)

FROM BONES

I AWOKE SLOWLY TO THE SOUNDS OF CHICKADEES SCREAMING. Their shriek was the aural approximation of the mid-air acrobatics, dive bombs, and lightning quick games of tag they played as they flitted through the humming forest. The chickadees paid no mind to the property lines that shatter the land around the lake into hundreds of pieces. These were documented on the black and white map hanging by the back door, with its columns of names and their corresponding property numbers littered, like a connect-the-dots drawing, across the image of the long lake. The birds understood only the borders between the air and the land, and the other one, dividing life from death.

The light in the bedroom was filtered through the forest canopy outside. I pulled on my jeans and the oversized plaid shirt I found in the mud room and stumbled through the curtain that led from the bedroom to the connected living room and dining room. I pulled open the yellow curtains as I went, and my sleep encrusted eyes were nearly blinded by the light reflecting off the grey-blue lake as it danced across the wood-panelled walls.

I walked to the kitchen and stood in front of the wood stove, opening the flue and spinning a handle that dropped the previous day's ashes into a hold, where they waited to be swept into a tin bucket and brought to the outhouse. Inside its steel belly I built a teepee of kindling, stuffed with balled newspaper. Beside it stood a log, in a good position to be dropped onto the fire once it got burning. Summer was ending, and every morning I followed this ritual to take the chill out of the high-ceilinged cottage.

My other morning ritual dragged me outside, where I noticed more orange and red leaves on the forest canopy than the day before. I followed the uneven path, over rock and wood chip, to a ten-foot-tall wood hut built of logs and seemingly held together by moss. Inside, the walls were painted a doctor's office shade of white and there was a sweet smell of excrement and ash. I pulled the clapboard door closed and, pulling down my jeans, sat on one of the two toilet seats.

"There's two of everything up here," I told a friend on the phone a week before, in my last communication with the city an hour's drive away. I had been up there alone for three weeks now, and was beginning to get a little lonesome. "Two stoves, two bedrooms, two sail boats, two cabins, two fridges—one for food and one for booze..." And now I realized I had missed yet another pair, two toilet seats in the outhouse. "One for you and one for your sweetie," was how one of my friends later solved the riddle.

It was just further proof of my theory that my grandfather hadn't merely set out to build a summer cottage for his five children. He was on a mission of much greater importance. My grandfather Miller was a religious man, one of the seven founding fathers of St. Stephen's Presbyterian Church. But for all his faith, he understood that all was not well and that eventually God's anger would raise the tides of the world once more. And so Grampy set out to build an ark. Knowing very well that in his day and age ark building was a hobby commonly frowned upon, especially among his upwardly mobile Scot immigrant friends and parishioners, he camouflaged it as a cottage.

Thus was born a summer home crammed full of everything needed for years at sea and the subsequent repopulation by Millers of the freshly baptized world. Numerous radios, sets of cutlery, woodworking tools, broken alarm clocks, dozens of fishing rods, glossy magazines and potboiler paperbacks were vital to the mission. It's difficult to imagine the five-room cottage he built as seafaring, held up as it is by stilts of cinder blocks, and hanging, as it does, precariously over a hill, but my grandfather's faith in God's providence was buoyant.

Times have changed and the cottage has now already waited a half century to be christened. The summers are dryer than ever. Now the city stretches closer to us, creeping further west along Highway 7 with each passing summer. As much a part of the present day scenery as the Holsteins, ruminating behind weather-beaten cordwood fences, are the billboard advertisements popping out of fields promising freedom of every variety. You can drown your sorrows in an 'unlabelled' beer while 'banking in your pyjamas,' and eating '100% beef patties' from a roadside chain.

The Richmond Bakery, the customary leg stretch, however, remains unchanged. Located at the halfway point from the city to the lake, it employs unimpressed, heavily made-up country high school girls who sling day old cookies and tough sugar doughnuts that, truth be told, aren't very good.

Across the 7 their boyfriends haunt the parking lot of the Beatrice convenience store, sitting in the flatbeds of pickup trucks borrowed from their mothers. These young men sport dirt-lip moustaches and wife-beater undershirts, blasting Hot 89.9 on their overtaxed car stereos. Their love of urban music somehow supersedes their rural upbringing.

From the bakery, the highway leads through one scenic town after another. Each can claim some manner of Eastern Ontario fame, be it for eighteenth-century military canals, discount coat factories, or a Hershey chocolate factory. Near one of these towns there's a road that, if you make a ninety-degree turn at the right moment, will deliver you onto a dirt road that leads you to where the Miller cottage sits waiting on the shore of one of the secluded bays of Otty Lake. But first there's the matter of a five minute drive into the brush, past stagnant bogs and crooked evergreens, along one of the most twisting, turning, climbing and descending roads ever designed by the necessity of the land.

In the late fifties my father and his brother Ian shared the ownership of a red Barracuda. When the humid valley heat drove them mental, they followed a simple plan of action. First, they would get tanked in the city, at the Ottawa House or the Diplomat. After last call they drove fast along the empty night roads that led to the cottage. They always made it to the dirt road, but without fail their hatchback would end up in one of the swamps next to a sharp turn. From the crash site they would walk in the rest of the way, swatting mosquitoes and worrying about how they would find someone to tow out the car next afternoon.

A daddy-long-legs crawled out of the toilet seat next to mine and continued climbing up the wall. I finished up and was walking back to the cottage when I heard something far off, over the hum of the calling birds and circling mosquitoes. It was the crackle and pop of wheels crawling across the gravel road. The sounds of the road got louder as it announced an arrival. Over the last rise I saw a vehicle crawling forth, a van, stout and dark blue. Once it climbed down the hill it turned off the road onto the property.

I stood by the woodpile and watched the approach until the van came to a rest. Pulling a baseball cap from my back pocket and onto my head, I shouted "How y'all doing?" as the doors opened and my friends emerged, stepping slowly out onto the forest floor carpeted with wind-fallen leaves.

The last time my friends paid me a visit here was on the birthday that sealed the worst year of my young life. It's a rare event for me these days to promote a concert, much less one in honour of something so trivial as my birthday. When I do, however, I try to do it somewhere as inconveniently located as possible. This policy whittles away the dilettantes and hangers-on, so that only the true hardcore will attend, usually my best friends.

The year had been bad for everyone. My mom and dad both lost their fathers and my mother struggled with the added burden of executing her father's estate, JB and I both fell victim to monumental heartbreak, and Jon suffered from an existential crisis. Everyone was struggling with the lives they had chosen. But now we were going to have a big purifying bonfire to burn off our fears.

First to arrive, the day of the party, was the car from Montreal. Johnny, patron saint of the Van Horne train yards, came up in the car with Poland's favourite son, Bartek. Johnny and I canoed across the bay in the fading light with Gaia, Bartek's family greyhound, who understands only Polish commands. The two of us were shirtless; my skin was lily white and Johnny's a deep shade of brown decorated with homemade tattoos of lightning bolts and electrical plugs. Our aluminum vessel teetered as Gaia shifted her weigh, lying down only after she deigned to understand my butchered Polish command of 'sit' (pronounced something like 'hotch').

Despite her liability to our seafaring mission, it was beautiful to watch the movement of her taut muscles once we reached the island, across the bay. She dove after every stick we threw and rolled with joy, scratching her back on a pile of snail shells. She ran across every inch of the island. "I bet she can smell every dog that's been here in the last twenty years," Johnny said as Gaia bounded from tree to tree across the mossy island.

I could see traces of every relation, friend, and lover that had passed through my grandfather's acre of land in the past fifty years. A swarm of humanity had climbed the hill, sunned on the raft. I saw them all for a moment, shimmering like light on the water. Some living, others passed on, all across the bay, and then I turned away.

Loon calls warbled across the darkening lake, the feathered family calling each other out, just as we would soon be singing to each other. The numbers of attendees swelled as night fell. Friends spilled in from every corner. Time became malleable and we served the mosquitoes a feast of young blood. Across from the deck, on the dock, a small group sat circled around the weak flame of a citronella candle, their faces painted with shadow, smoke, and talk.

Jeremy set up the drum kit, battered and sparkling on the dusty carpet in front of the stone fireplace just past sunset. Mike constructed a makeshift vocal PA, by turning a floor lamp into a mike stand, then running a patch cord over the rafter beams into a tiny practice amp sitting on the mantle.

As the band set up everyone cleared out of the crowded cottage and sat on the deck, which had no railing. To this day I think it's a miracle, with all the people and all the booze consumed, that no one has yet fallen onto the shore below, laden with rocks as well as rusty rebar and cracked concrete left over from Grampy's half-assed attempt at straightening out the shoreline, circa 1967. I stared at the rebar, imagining the blood flowing from a punctured body, and wondered how fast the lockjaw would set in...

Finally, Jeremy yelled from behind his kit "We're ready to play," and we pulled ourselves from the green plastic patio chairs, and walked up the hill, through the yellow trimmed door, to find a place in the mis-matched cottage.

Mike stepped to the microphone, 'feelings' written across his guitar in white letraset. Mike's songs may be about just that, the old feelings of love and uncertainty, but the lyrics are cliche free.

I first heard him play some years ago at one of the hushed concerts in my hometown's art galleries. I was sixteen, and all that I could understand about his songs were that they weren't Ottawa Hardcore. They were filled with silences and melodies, instead of feedback and opaque lyricisms. But as I grew from a precocious teenager into whatever I am now I grew into his songs, or they grew into me. Now I find myself holding back tears whenever I hear the him sing a cappella the last song of that night, its simple refrain "my love is a bell / it won't sing unless you ring it," his voice clear and strong.

"Skinny dipping!" someone yelled once Mike finished and we tumbled down the hill in a fit of tearing off clothes, and swam into the night. In the lake there are no horizons, just heads bobbing out of water. In the water all those things that chased us lose our trail, everything that is heavy becomes light, and we are as safe as my grandmother on her horse Nelly at age two, when she and her mother sat in Lake Porcupine as fire claimed everything around them.

Here we are in the lake in the night, and the deluge has yet to claim our world. Up in the ark someone is handing my father a shot of vodka and a breeze disrupts the smoke from the fire pit. Over the mantle hangs a piece of whitewashed driftwood that resembles a fish in motion and below it sits a flat stone with the word REMEMBER carved across it. Yes, remember those who have passed, and those who remain, held in the palm of the night's massive hand.

(Ghost Pine #7: Blood, 2003)

MAGPIES

WHEN I WAS EIGHT YEARS OLD, I MOVED TO EDMONTON, ALBERTA, the gateway to Canada's mythological Far North.

I cried. I know this is true because I was leaving behind everything I had ever known: an army of extended family and the house whose nooks and crannies (including a few in the backyard cedars) had raised me. I was also leaving behind my grandmother who lived five blocks from my house and whom, it's quite possible, I loved more than anyone else I'd known in my short life.

Edmonton had ample cloudless sky, it was almost like a

gem you could mount on a ring. The only house I had known until then had been cut from the bolt of cloth of uniform suburbia, and was thus exactly the same as every third house the length of our street, and many other houses built in 1971 by the Minto corporation. The house my parents found in Edmonton had been built by a maverick contractor named Don. He had a friend who worked in the carpet business, so the floor of every room was hidden by luscious shag carpeting. The kitchen had slightly shorter carpet and only one of the two bathrooms was shagged. The other was covered in wood and housed a sauna that could fit three people.

While, in my peripheral Ottawa suburb, downtown was a distant rumour, it was close to this carpet house. The mid-sized banking towers of the Prairies could be seen from the park at the end of the street, glittering like the dreams of cowboy financiers. A few blocks from my bedroom, Vietnamese triads were busy shooting each other gangland-style in the alleys and split-levels. I remember hearing of one such gangland shoot up not too far from my house and thinking "Holy shit!"

But the proximity to downtown had its plus side. Dad made it home from work at twenty after five everyday and, unlike in the suburbs, long cracked alleys ran behind the yards of all the houses. All kinds of life spilled back there. Hobby mechanics pulled up the doors of their dilapidated stucco garages. More often than not, the interior would be wallpapered with full-colour pages ripped from *Playboy* and I would walk by slow, trying to catch a glimpse.

There was life everywhere in the alley—tomcats clawing each other to bits (like our pet, Minou #1), and dogs yapping at them. Raccoons searched the trash for food by moonlight and by day vagrants wandered the same route, looking for empty bottles. I watched them pass by as I shot hoops on the basketball net Don had installed for his kid.

Sometimes there was a little bit too much life. In winter, the magpies began cawing long before the lazy sun would start climbing into the sky.

"I shot three of them yesterday." Every morning disgruntled

Edmontonians called into a show on the talk radio station to tell how many magpies they had shot the previous day. We precious Easterners were horrified by this Wild West-style shooting in the streets. But it was my grandfather, old Lester, visiting over Christmas, who put it best.

"The birds are just doin' what we're all doin': complainin' about the goddamn weather. It's tellin' the truth, that ain't no reason to kill it!"

One of the other joys of living on the fringe of the city centre was the cultural life. What's culture to an eight-year-old, you ask? Well, it's everything. For instance, my folks had no qualms about setting me and my twelve-year-old brother free and unsupervised at the convention centre when the comic book convention came around. As a result, my brother took a piss in the urinal next to the great comic mogul Stan Lee. Whether he said "Excelsior!" or not as he zipped up his fly, my brother doesn't remember.

The main branch of the Edmonton Public Library was a six-storey relic from the days when Alberta was flush with oil money, before the big slump of the eighties. To get there we had to drive the family minivan through an aberration of urban planning known as the Rat Hole. It featured a jackrabbit zig of a turn before diving into the tunnel, and an equally jarring zag to get out of it. Several years ago this atrocity completely filled with water during a tornado season blow-out. Currently, I read, the Rat Hole has been dismantled so that contractors could build 'loft-style condos' over it. O Lost!

At the library, in the basement kids' section I searched through a selection of tattered and worn four-colour comic books, picking the best ones and checking them out. Upstairs my brother learned that he could take out hip-hop LPs for two weeks at a time. He unearthed Digital Underground, LL Cool J, Cold Cut (that James Brown remix), Run DMC—even the first record by the controversial 2 Live Crew, from the fourth floor A.V. department.

Comic books' distortion of the world seems to be an apt metaphor for those twelve inches my brother listened to. The world in those rhymes was just a little bit bigger, brighter and a lot less nuanced in a way that an eight-year-old could really get into.

My father occasionally came downstairs, into our basement rec room to complain that the 808 thump of "My Adidas" was so loud that it was interfering with his jazz upstairs. Inevitably he would make some passing remark on the repetitive nature of the music and the poor quality of the lyrics. We would invoke Lester's one-time defence of the winter magpies. "Dad, they're just telling the truth. That's no reason to hate them."

While I never immersed myself in hip-hop as an adolescent, it had already saturated me as a child. The rhymes to Kurtis Blow's "Back By Popular Demand" are lodged in the same lobe of childhood arcana that houses my knowledge of the secret identities of every superhero in the Marvel Universe.

Maybe it's because of this that sometimes, mostly when I'm high and sitting on one of the shiny metal benches at Lionel-Groulx Metro, waiting on a train, I feel the weight of my notebook in my little black backpack and think, "Didn't Q-Tip write a rhyme about keeping his poetry in his back pack?" And I hope silently that when Rammelzee, Rakim and the Jigga are inducted into the English cannon, sympathetic critics of the day will look back on my work and call me the slowest, worst-rhyming MC in history. But an MC nonetheless. And I smile because I'm fucked up and here comes my train.

(Ghost Pine #8: Wolf, 2004)

INTERVIEW BY CIARA XYERRA, FEBRUARY 2007

HOW DID YOU GET INVOLVED IN ZINES AND DO IT YOURSELF PUBLISHING?

In the fall of 1994 I was in the tenth grade and heard that some of the kids in grade thirteen were going to start an independent publication. The year before, the school had censored all the content in the school newspaper and then cancelled it altogether. I went to the inaugural meeting in the backyard of one of the older students, there were about twenty of us and after some discussion we decided to start a zine. That was *Saccharine*. Although it was ostensibly an arena for us to comment freely on the goings on at our high school, we never wrote about school at all. Instead *Saccharine* was one of the million crappy zines featuring rants, record reviews and bad collage layouts that proliferated in the mid-nineties. Eventually those in the graduating class became more interested in their university applications and our zine petered out. One of the coolest things that came out of doing that zine was that it gave me confidence enough to ask Sloan's drummer if I could interview him. We sat out on the back porch and I wrote down what he said on bar napkins. All I remember is that he told me SST Records changed his life.

I became friends with Adam, an older student who wrote record reviews for *Saccharine* under the nom de plume "Relic." He was the president of the student body but also into hardcore. We started going to shows at Ottawa punkhouse 5 Arlington. At this time our town had one of the best hardcore scenes in North America. Shotmaker, Uranus and the lesser known but no less mind-blowing Okara played every week. The bands were wicked, but I was equally inspired by the community around them. At every show people were selling zines and records that they had made. From the outside it seemed like everyone in the small scene had their role to play, everyone was doing something to make the greater whole happen. One of the first zines I bought at 5A was *Mooh/Meuh*, a bilingual political zine by two punks named Pete and Chantal. It inspired me to go vegetarian.

At the end of the summer of 1995, Adam left to go to university in Vancouver and by the winter 5A had shut down. I was lonely and felt that the Ottawa scene I took so much pride in was falling apart and that I needed to participate in it before it was gone. In March 1996 I published the first issue of *Otaku*, the zine that would eventually become *Ghost Pine*. A few months after I had sent them a copy, *HeartattaCk* published a positive review of my zine. I would like to thank whoever wrote that review because it really did mean the world to me. I spent the summer after grade ten writing letters and sending away for zines, getting them in my mailbox weeks and months later.

WHAT IS YOUR PROCESS LIKE?

First I get an idea for a story. Next I think about it for a length of time, anywhere from a few days to a few years. Then I write a draft in my journal. Making something out of nothing is, of course, the funnest part. After writing a draft I type it up in my computer. I've found that it's a lot easier to keep track of stories if they get typed up sooner rather than later, even if in the typing I'm forced to realize they weren't as good as I thought. I let the story sit in my hard drive for a while before coming back to edit it. Sometimes I write new parts to the story in my journal and then type them in. Editing is the bulk of my writing process and often the most painful. It takes forever, but is totally worth it. I've spent thousands and thousands of hours sitting with computers or pieces of paper editing stories.

Once a critical mass of stories are near enough to completion I kick it into high gear and spend all my free time editing for a month or so until I decide the zine is done. After this I print it out and do cut and paste lay out for a few hours. I chose to use a standard format for the zine because I don't like spending too much time cutting and pasting.

I used to hand-write the zine, but to spend all my time copy-editing on a computer and then make typos while inscribing it was too heartbreaking. Some may argue that hand-written zines are more intimate but my aesthetic criteria as a zine reader is based solely on the quality of the writing.

HOW DO YOU THINK THE ZINE COMMUNITY OR THE PROCESS OF MAKING ZINES HAS CHANGED SINCE YOU'VE BEEN INVOLVED?

I don't know if this is happening elsewhere in North America, but here in Montreal I've had lots of luck with giving readings over the last five years. Lots of people come out, many of whom would never pick up a zine. Audiences are quiet but know to laugh in the right places. I think readings are a good way for misanthropic zine writers to connect with the larger underground community. People are hungry for stories.

ARE YOU "OUT" TO PEOPLE IN YOUR LIFE AS A ZINESTER? HOW DO YOU EXPLAIN IT TO PEOPLE WHO DON'T UNDERSTAND?

My friends and family know, but I don't go around telling people that I do a zine. I'm more low key than that. My zine is a pretty soft sell to normal people since for the last five years it has been modelled on the tried and true medium of the short story collection. More difficult is explaining that the stories in my small collections are all true. People have a hard time believing something well-written could also be true.

WHAT DO YOU LIKE BEST ABOUT THE ZINE WORLD?

I'm something of an anxious person so it's nice to have a reason to run errands and make to-do lists. I really love the minutia of it, packing up letters and walking to the post office, going to the copy shop and fighting with the photocopiers, etc. I also enjoy the fact that my labours have made me a member of a secret society. My friends who began making zines ten years ago and are still at it today are connected to me in a way similar to blood relation. We've shared experiences that we can only talk about with each other. And of course it goes without saying that I love the constant stream of amazing writing and art that comes out of the zine world.

WHAT ADVICE MIGHT YOU HAVE FOR SOMEONE WHO IS NEW TO THE ZINE COMMUNITY?

Order and read as many zines as possible. Then read books, read the newspaper, read everything you can. Also magazines. Be humble but brave. Write letters to people whose zine you like, they'll appreciate it even if they don't reply. Ninety percent of writing is editing. Get other people to read your stuff before you print it. Don't be angry if they give you criticism, you have to listen to them if you ever want to get any better. Be patient most of the time and frantic a little bit of the time. Learn by doing, no one in zines does anything the same as anyone else because everyone had to figure it out for themselves. It takes a lot of time.

Nepean writers lead the zine scene in Canada

zINECORE '98

Otaku, 1996

Otaku Trust, 1996

Otaku #3, 1997

Otaku #4, 1999

Otaku #5, 1999

Ghost Pine #6, 2001

Ghost Pine #7: Blood, 2003

Ghost Pine #8: Wolf, 2004

Ghost Pine #9: Bees, 2005

Ghost Pine #10: Wires, 2006

Ghost Pine #11: Crows, 2007

Negative Capability #1, 2008

Interview with Sloan drummer Andrew Scott in *Saccharine #1*, 1994

My office, 1997

2002

2004

2004

2006

2008

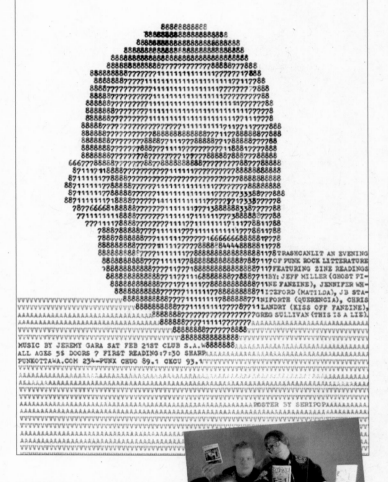

Top: 2004 (poster by Seripop)
Right: Promo photo for Trash Can Lit, 2004

Making *Ghost Pine #8*, 2004

Mailing out *Ghost Pine* #10, 2007

Reading at the Greasy Goose, 2008

Biography

Jeff Miller has published the zine *Ghost Pine* since 1996. His writing has also appeared in *The 2nd Hand*, *Broken Pencil*, *Zine Yearbook* and *The Art of Trespassing* (Invisible Publishing).

Born and raised in Ottawa, he has lived in Montreal for the past decade, where he continues to write.